anything's
POSSIBLE!

anything's POSSIBLE!

Curtis J. Steen

Edited by W. A. Newman

CJS
Training & Consulting

ANYTHING'S POSSIBLE!
Curtis J. Steen

CJS Training & Consulting
An affiliate of
Truby Achievement Center
P.O. Box 1440
Mt. Shasta, California 96067
Tel; Fax; Pager: 800-792-1262 (toll free)

Find us on the World Wide Web at:
www.soaringeaglesdivision.com
www.trubyachievementcenter.com

Copyright © 2003 by Curtis J. Steen
and the Truby Achievement Center

Cover design by Dan Bunter

Interior design and illustrations:
William A. Newman and
Wordsmiths Marketing
530-235-0953
info@wordsmithsmarketing.com

Colophon
This book was created with Adobe InDesign 2.0 on a Macintosh G3. The body text is set in Adobe Garamond; illustration captions are set in Helvetica Neue.

Notice of Rights
All rights reserved. No part of this book may be reproduced or transmitted in any form or by any means, electronic, mechanical, photocopying, recording, or otherwise, without the prior written permission of the publisher. For information on getting permission or reprints and excerpts, contact Curtis J. Steen.

Notice of Liability
The information in this book is distributed on an "as is" basis without warranty. While every precaution has been taken in the preparation of this book, neither the author, the editor, or the Truby Achievement Center shall have any liability to any person or entity with respect to any loss or damage caused or alleged to be caused directly or indirectly by any information in this book.

ISBN 0-9741598-0-8
Printed and bound in the United States of America by LSI

Dedication

Dedicated to a person I have always looked up to, my awesome brother and business partner, Ryan Russell Steen, an individual who always seems to be one step ahead of the crowd.

Contents

Dedication v
Appreciation ix
Acknowledgements xi
Forward xiii
Introduction: What do you want? xvii
Chapter 1: How to get started right the first time 25
Chapter 2: With that mind set, sit down and plan your life 49
Chapter 3: Keep focused and revisit your plan daily 83
Chapter 4: Choose someone fun to help you along your journey .. 95
Chapter 5: Don't just walk, leap to success 101
Chapter 6: Obstacles can be easy 109
Chapter 7: Now, it's about action 137
About the Author 142

Appreciation

I would like to express my gratitude to Bill and Joann Truby, co-founders of the Truby Achievement Center, for their generosity in allowing me to use some of their concepts set forth in this book.

Bill Truby, M.A., MFCC has been teaching personal, interpersonal and organizational success strategies for the past 20 years. His teachings and concepts, some of which are taught in this book, work.

Joann Truby is an experienced consultant, speaker, trainer, facilitator, and leadership coach. She has been a consultant to scores of businesses helping them be successful.

I also want to thank and express my gratitude to the many other people who have taught me ideas that I have implemented in this book.

Thank you!

x

Acknowledgements

There are many people I need to thank. These are the people have made an impact in my life.

I want to thank my father Clifford Steen for being so supportive, amazing in perspective and knowledge, and giving me so much in life. I am so lucky to be your son.

I want to thank my grandparents Russ and Carol Dillender for supporting me through tough times and allowing me get my feet on the ground. Their kindness shines.

I want to thank Jack and Dorothy Steen for making me laugh, caring so much, and playing golf with me.

I want to thank Dennis Rippey for taking me in like a son. It meant so much to me in difficult times.

I want to thank my brother Ryan Steen for being such a protective and supportive brother. There were many times he shared his great perspective on how I could be better.

I want to thank my mother Joann, and her husband Bill, for supporting me financially, helping me write, and encouraging me with this venture.

I want to thank Jennifer Borer, an amazing young lady who continually gives me so much love, support, and commitment.

And thank you to my editor, Will Newman, for his help in making one of my dreams a reality.

Lastly, and most importantly, thank *you* for reading this book.

≈Forward≈

When I met Curtis I was surprised, pleased and puzzled. Surprised to find such energy directed toward values and perspectives that were way beyond his years. Pleased to note that his beliefs and perspectives perpetuated him beyond the moment—he was planning out his life. Puzzled to find this kind of focus in a man his age. At that time he was only twenty years old.

Over time I learned that his beliefs, perspectives, ethics and values were real. They went to the very core of his being. And he brought them to his mission in life—to touch the lives of others and make a positive difference in those lives. I saw him carry that mission, along with his values, into every part of his life, from the football field, to the classroom, to his work, to his everyday interactions with people. He was, and is, unwavering.

I've watched Curtis learn how to follow his dream. When he was younger he could talk with great enthusiasm about reaching the top of the mountain. And he could see a first step he could take. But it was the long, uphill path between that first step and the top of the mountain that eluded him. He has learned how to create that path, however. This book is evidence of that.

His burning desire to write this book pleased me. He believed this is one of the best ways to touch many lives. And it is. When he would talk about his book, however, he could see many people reading it, but he didn't have the path to make it happen. As he grew in perspective and experience, he learned how to connect the beginning step with the end goal. When that happened, this book happened.

My connection with Curtis has been filled with joy. He has been an inspiration to me on many occasions, not the least of which has been the writing of this book. As I write this forward I reveal to you, and to Curtis, the inspirational nudge he has given me. His writing of this book inspires me to continue my writing.

You see, Curtis and I have many similar beliefs, desires and goals. Our mission in life is the same. I only wish I knew when I was his age what he knows now. I see incredible achievements for him in the future.

I mentioned the joy that has surrounded my relationship with Curtis. Part of that joy has come from his incessant desire to learn. He is constantly asking me questions. He hungers to learn, to grow, to apply his learning to his life, and to teach others what he has learned.

There are a number of concepts in this book I have developed and have been teaching for over twenty-five years. Curtis took the concepts, began practicing them in his life, distilled his experience and information into something simple and usable by others, and then wrote about them in this book. I admire that.

Take, for example, the concept of developing a healthy self-esteem that Curtis writes about. When I began teaching this concept over twenty-five years ago it would take me a few hours to teach it. Curtis has taken the concept and made it meaningful and useful within a few pages. He has made it easy to understand and put into practice.

Curtis has studied from a wide variety of leaders. His self-motivation to do this is incredible. While others his age would be out for the good time, Curtis manages to have a good time *and* create the time for his tireless regime of learning. You will see the results of this study reflected in this book.

There are many sources of wisdom and knowledge Curtis used to form the teachings in this book. That is what makes the concepts herein seem well beyond his years of experience. I know, however, that he has completely and deeply put into practice every concept he writes about here. You will see this demonstrated clearly as he reflects on his life of twenty-six years of experiences to illustrate the concepts.

There is youthfulness to his book. In the editing, I encouraged him to keep that spirit. It is something that is hard to replicate when you are older. Now, in this writing, this youthfulness wasn't created or conjured, it was simply captured. I can't wait for Curtis to read this when he is fifty years old and be inspired by his own pen.

Curtis has been working with my wife and me in the Truby Achievement Center for over two years. He leads our Soaring Eagles Division. It is the division of our company dedicated to helping young people learn what they didn't or couldn't learn in school. Curtis teaches them how to set goals, how to be confident, how to take life's difficulties and turn them into steppingstones of learning toward a better tomorrow. I am proud to have him as a part of our team. I am proud of his accomplishments. I am proud of this book. To me, Curtis exemplifies the ultimate Soaring Eagle.

My pride and joy have multi-dimensions, however. Not only is Curtis a great team member and a great leader of the Soaring Eagles Division, he is also my wife's son and my stepson. My pride and my joy are only surpassed by my love. I trust this book will teach you his secrets to a successful life and that you will duplicate that success in your life.

Bill Truby
Mount Shasta, California

~INTRODUCTION~

What Do You Want from Your Life?

I was fourteen years old. I can remember vividly attending the seminar like it was yesterday. John C. Maxwell, Jim Dornan, Skip Ross, Zig Ziglar, and a few other presenters were speaking about how to be successful in life and in business. I was on the edge of my seat. I cried, I laughed, and I was pumped up throughout the entire event. That seminar inspired and encouraged me to want to become a better person. It inspired and encouraged me to seek more out of life … to become a "bigger and better" person.

How about you? Do you want to have a bigger and better life? Do you want more in your life and more out of your life?

I hope your answer is "Yes" otherwise you wouldn't have this book in your hand. Or, maybe you don't know for sure if you want anything else and you just picked up this book for fun. If that's the case, my hope is that this book will inspire you to go beyond your present level of achievement … to strive to find levels of success you thought possible only in your dreams.

I often hear people say, "I am content with life. I am fine where I am in life. I don't want to accomplish anything else. I don't need anything more. My attitude is fine."

This attitude is fine if that is what you want and you want to stay that way, but hopefully you want more from life and want to be better at it. Now, if you are saying these things because you think you *can't* achieve something, or you *don't deserve* something, or you are nervous about something, don't let that happen!

Many wise people have said, "You can do anything you want … if you first put your mind to it." And that's true. But you first have to know how to go about it.

If you want more in life (meaning more happiness, knowing where you want to go and be, and being more effective with what you want), this book will help you find out exactly what you need to do to accomplish that goal.

Do you want changes in your life and not to live in fear?

That one seminar in San Diego, California, made a huge impact on me and in my life. I can remember watching those speakers influence people's lives for the better. As they spoke, I immediately thought that I wanted to influence others like that someday. I got pumped up as I thought of speaking in front of 10,000 people on leadership and personal development.

"Wouldn't that be awesome?" I thought to myself.

For me that was a great thought. But, the question is, "What do *you* love? What do *you* want to accomplish in your life?"

Speaking in front of people is what I wanted, but I had one problem … and that drawback was fear. I was frightened about speaking in front of crowds at that time. And you know what? I have never gotten rid of that fear. But I have learned how to lessen its influence over me. I am still nervous today when I speak in public, but I have chosen to give seminars anyway. I would rather live my dream of being on stage to influence others than live life based on my fear.

Why am I telling you this? To help you overcome your fear, if you have fear, and to do what *you* want and love. Wouldn't that be awesome?

You should never give power to a fear that holds you back from living the life that you want or love. If you want it, go get it. This book will help you to overcome your fears and other obstacles so you can get what you want.

Do you have a life purpose?

While attending that life-changing seminar, I was able to find my life purpose. As I watched the speakers on stage, it came to me. I knew then what I wanted to accomplish in my life. I wanted to make a positive difference in people's lives. And I was going to do this by being a motivational and leadership speaker like the people I saw on stage that day. I had found my life purpose.

This book is designed to help you find your life purpose and show you how to live out your life purpose <u>every single day</u>.

What kind of effort do you need?

Ever since I could remember, I thought it would be great to write and publish a book like this: a motivational book to help others.

What kind of work ethic did I need to accomplish this book?

I started writing this book when I was 15 years old. I would file away information, stories, and quotes so I could have enough information for when I was skilled enough to actually write the book. Now I am 26. It took me 11 years of little steps along the way consistently striving for my goal to accomplish writing this book. Persistence was vital in accomplishing my goals. And it is just as important in reaching your goals. Without it you *will* give up. But with persistence, anything is possible.

Life is an endless process, and so is success. It's the day in and day out activities that lead to your accomplishments.

I have learned from many people in my life—the people who have been my mentors—that the more you prepare yourself for your upcoming battles, the greater your chances of success. You must prepare yourself today so you can succeed tomorrow. Success takes time and persistent effort; so make sure you are patient and look continuously toward your goal. *There are no short cuts to success.*

Our mutual goal: For you to get the tools you need to be more effective

My purpose in writing this book should be the same you have in picking it up, that is for you to learn the tools you need to be more effective in achieving your goals and to turn your dreams into today's reality.

How you set your goals is as important as almost anything else you do to attain your goals. This is so because how you set those goals will determine if you will be successful or not.

I tried to achieve goals in two ways. One way to set goals was to only think about them, which was a mistake. The other, successful way, was to write them down. Don't make the same mistake I did. When I only thought about my goals, I didn't accomplish much and I was not focused enough. However, when I wrote down my goals, I achieved more and overcame my challenges more quickly and more easily than when I only thought about them. That is the truth. And that is the important first step in accomplishing your goals.

Many successful people have said that when you write down your goals and review them on a regular basis, you *always* do better than when you simply think about them. So, by planning your future in this way, you develop alignment and focus. By doing this you will save time because you will achieve your goals more quickly.

Setting goals is simple—but not easy. That is why few people are successful in getting what they want.

There are two core reasons people are successful in achieving their goals. These reasons affect other goal-achieving factors as well.

First, it comes down to what goals you set and how realistic those goals are.

Many people do not get where they really want to go because they set goals that are unrealistic. They set them too high. They set goals that are not achievable. It's like people thinking they can put something on the moon when they first should think about putting something on top of a mountain or even on top of a small hill first.

It is the small steps, aligned with what you want, that produce the big outcomes. I was not successful in a previous career because I set goals that were too high. These unrealistic goals actually hindered me and held me back.

Secondly, it comes down to your belief system.

Do you really believe you can do it?

"If you believe you can, you will. If you believe you can't, you won't."

To get where you want to go, you need to take action that takes you towards your goals. And action comes from your belief that you *can* do it. If you believe, your actions come next and you will keep on persisting because you want it. In elementary school I didn't believe in myself, and I didn't do well. When I finally believed in myself, I did very well. I received A's and B's in high school and received an average of a B at U.C. Davis, simply because of my belief in myself.

Without belief you are doomed to disaster and you will not achieve what you want. I know this sounds really harsh, but it is true.

Sometimes you need to refocus

As we go through life, we can get caught up in our daily, busy tasks. Sometimes we get so busy we need to step back and plan or refocus on where we want to go. Believe it or not, planning does save time. It creates more time in the future.

I believe this book will help you set more effective goals that will then create a higher success rate in your life. In my life I have read many books and I have learned many things from them, but more importantly I have tried to apply them *every day of my life*. I have succeeded often, but I have also made many mistakes. After you read this book I hope you can implement some or all of my ideas and learn from my experiences where it will help you the best. I promise you will see and feel a difference if you take anything from this book.

You will have challenges and struggles because—as you have undoubtedly noticed—life does not always go the way you want or expect it to go. Struggles and challenges are part of the process of learning, growing, and living. Learn to like, or at least accept, them.

How to use this book

Let me paint an overall picture of what this book will teach you. First you have to realize the importance of your "Why" and your "What". You need to make the decision on why you want what you want. You also have to believe in it while making a strategic plan to get there. And if need be, you need to make necessary changes to your plan. Then, you need to find a coach who will help you along your journey, and more importantly, help you enjoy the process of getting there. Then you can't forget about planning how you will overcome your roadblocks, while developing actions that are consistent and persistent towards your goals.

Success is a process and not a quick fix or a one-day shot, so I recommend reading this book in the following way.

First, read all the way through the book and acquire a sense of what is being taught or refreshed for you.

After you have read it that first time, go back through the book slowly. Read the first chapter, and let it sit for a couple of days so you can implement it into your daily routine.

After you have incorporated the first chapter into your daily routine, read the next chapter. Let it sit for a couple of days to understand it. Then implement that content into your daily routine, too.

Then read the next chapter, let it sit for a couple of days so you can implement it in your daily routine. Keep on following this structure with each chapter until you finish the book.

There are seven chapters in the book. If you follow my suggestions, it could take you approximately 4 to 6 weeks to go through. Go at your own pace. Spend a day or a month on one chapter if you want to.

Use however *you* learn best to get the most out of this book. This book is for you to get the most out of it and to challenge you to do more in your life.

Hopefully you will enjoy using this book as much as I enjoyed writing it. Please send your comments and stories to me because hearing about your success fulfills my joy and passion. Maybe the next book will be a collaboration of stories from people who have succeeded because of this book. Wouldn't that be awesome?

Lets do it!

CURTIS J. STEEN

Chapter 1

"How to get started right ... ... the first time"   25

In this chapter you will learn:
- Why it is important to believe;
- What healthy self-esteem means;
- How to develop a mind set of "Possibility Thinking;"
- Why your attitude is so important;
- Getting to know your "Why."

I was in the 2nd grade walking out of a classroom towards my special teacher. She wanted me for something that I thought was embarrassing and degrading. As I was walking out of the classroom, I was nervous, scared, embarrassed, and wanted to cry. The students were laughing at me and saying mean things about me. Things like "He is dumb" and "He needs special help."

Why were they saying this?

The students were laughing because I went to this teacher who was helping me with my stuttering and reading deficiency. I was not a good reader, and I was a slow learner. That is why they were saying these bad things about me.

In elementary school I was not succeeding in many of my classes. Because of this, my teachers wanted to put me in special-ed. The regular students who could read stayed in the regular English class. I was the only one who went to the special teacher. I envied the students who could read. I wanted to be like them.

This special teacher was going to determine if I would be put into special-ed or not. When they decided I should be put in special-ed, my parents fought for me. My mother, Joann, had a plan. Instead of my having to go into special-ed, she home schooled me.

So, how come I wasn't doing well in school?

I had a great work ethic and tried hard, but it just wasn't working for me. It got worse and worse as time went on because more and more students made fun of me. Because of this, I thought I was dumb. Their comments could have destroyed me, but I had the strength to have a good spirit and to keep on trying. I also had a great plan to succeed in life. My problem was not a lack of spirit; my problem was:

> **"I had no belief that I could do it,
> and I had a very low self-esteem."**

I thought I was "dumb" because I couldn't do what other kids my age could and because everyone else (except my parents) said I couldn't do it. It was not until later, after being home schooled by my awesome mom, that I realized I really could do the work.

Before *you* start planning what you want in life, it is vital to develop a strong belief in yourself, to develop a positive attitude, to develop a healthy self-esteem, and to develop the mind set of "Possibility Thinking".

Let's talk about each of these in detail.

First, a strong belief

At first, I had only one-half of what I needed for success. I had a good work ethic and tried very hard, but I did not have the belief that I could do it. As an individual, *you first need to believe.* Believe in yourself because your beliefs dictate your actions.

Why is it vital to have a strong belief in yourself? Many leadership speakers say that believing is half the battle. When you believe, you are half way there. A man or a woman with belief cannot be denied. But, if you don't believe you can do it, you won't. This I promise.

In my days of school, starting from 4th grade and on, I started getting very good grades, actually getting as high as 4.0 in high school and an average of a 3.0 in college.

Why?

Because I finally believed I could do it. It is extraordinary what you can do when you believe.

So, how do *you* believe?

First, you make a choice that you are a powerful person who can do anything you put your mind to. I am talking about having a healthy belief in yourself—not a boastful or arrogant belief but one that comes across to others that you are a person with belief in what you can do. Belief is kind of like the wind, you feel it but you can't see it.

If you just can't make the decision to believe, you can find the ability to do it from somewhere else in your life. I personally found my belief in my scholastic abilities from another area of my life, how God believes in me. I transferred that kind of belief to how I needed to believe in myself regarding school. If you are like I was, you can transfer your experience of success from a successful area of life to another.

A relevant football story

In 1997-2000, I attended University of California at Davis and majored in Managerial Economics. I was a student-athlete all through high school and into college. As an athlete, I learned many core concepts about life. I learned about teamwork, belief, commitment, focus and much more.

Bob Biggs, my head coach for the Aggie's, always emphasized how important it was to believe. He always made statements like these: "Without belief, we will not win. Without faith, we are doomed."

Isn't that so true? Without belief, you can't accomplish what you set out to do, and without hope for the future, you won't be excited about life.

It is very important to have belief because it gives you confidence. But remember, <u>confidence with humility</u> is important. Nobody likes a person who arrogantly struts around. With over-confidence, you will come across as boastful or arrogant; so you need a healthy confidence tempered with humility.

Belief will also help you develop courage to go into the unknown. Courage will then help you make that first step when the future is sketchy or scary. But with a strong, healthy belief in yourself, you will have courage to take that first step. Have belief in yourself, as God believes in you and wants the best for you.

A great Bible story on belief

In the book of Genesis, there is a story about how Joseph, son of Jacob, went against all odds. His brothers threw him down a well to die. Soon, some people found him and rescued him but only to sell him into slavery in Egypt for many years of his life. But he kept his belief that he could be great and he would be free.

After all these challenges in life, he became a valued adviser to the pharaoh. He never blamed God, but he believed that God had control of his life. God put Joseph in a position of power with Pharaoh because he never stopped believing, just as we need to constantly believe in ourselves.

Second, develop a healthy self-esteem

Self-esteem can help build your belief; so later in this book you'll learn from the co-founders of the Truby Achievement Center how to have a healthy self-esteem. The Truby Achievement Center's teaching about self-esteem have been very important in formulating my personal life experiences and thoughts.

What is a healthy self-esteem, and how can it directly influence us? Wouldn't it be great not to get upset when someone says something bad about you … to be able to take criticism? That can happen with a healthy self-esteem.

When we are born, we began relating to a Dominant Parent Influence (DPI). From that DPI we learned a standard of acceptance that determined if we felt accepted or not. This means that <u>all the input</u> we had during our early years established our self-esteem. There are two forms of this standard of acceptance:

1) Conditional acceptance, and
2) Unconditional acceptance

What is conditional acceptance?

Conditional acceptance gives the message that if you do well, you are a good person. It tells you that you are only valuable if others tell you that you are or that you are valuable only because you did a good job. Conditional acceptance is based on performance. You are accepted when you do something well and not accepted when you do something "bad."

What is unconditional acceptance?

Unconditional acceptance gives you the message that it does not matter whether you do "bad" or "good;" you are a still valuable person. If you do something "bad," it does not mean you are not a valuable person. Of course, if you do something that's not your best, you still need to take responsibility for it. But you are *still* a valuable person even when you make a wrong decision. If you were getting spanked for doing something wrong, you are not getting punished because you are bad as a person. You just did something that was not appropriate. It is important to understand the difference between the two.

If people tell you that you are mean or are a jerk, that doesn't determine who you are as a person. You are still a valuable person even if you get in trouble for doing something that is not good. You just made a bad decision or choice.

What I am saying is this: If you do something bad or if you do something good and are noticed for it, you should take it in just as "input." You don't need someone to say you did well to make you happy. You know anyway that you are a happy person regardless. Yes, good input feels good, but you need to watch this because if you place too much faith in positive input, you can be devastated when people say negative things about you.

If you move that mountain by 3 o'clock, it means you have done a good job but not that you are a good person simply because you moved that mountain. You just have a good work ethic.

Unconditional acceptance sounds better ... and it is ... but most of us were raised with conditional acceptance.

When I was in school, conditional acceptance was my overriding problem. I did not have any belief in myself because students would make fun of me and tell me I was stupid. This did not foster a strong, positive belief in myself.

Why were most of us raised with conditional acceptance?

Most parents just don't know any better. They are doing what they learned from their parents and doing the best they can to raise their children.

My parents raised my brother Ryan and me with conditional acceptance. If we did well we got recognized positively, and if we did poorly we got recognized for doing poorly. We got recognized for when we did awesomely in sports and in school. But when we didn't do as well, we felt very insecure and devalued.

I tried to excel because I got attention from it. My brother, on the other hand, did the "bad" things, but he still got attention, in this case, with disciplinary actions. And sometimes when we did something bad, we got the message that we were "bad" kids when we were disciplined.

I found out that when I did the right things, I got praised like I was an awesome person because of my actions, not because I was a valuable person. I felt more valuable when I did something well than when I did something poorly. I got praised when I got good grades, but I felt dumb when I got a bad grade.

I decided to learn from my brother. He would drink and get in big trouble. So I thought I wouldn't, and family members said that I was such a smart man for not drinking. They would say, "Curtis is such a great kid. He doesn't drink."

Today, if I were to take a sip of alcohol, people would look at me and say, "Why is he drinking? Something must be wrong." People are still conditionally accepting me in regards to alcohol; they think it's honorable for me not to drink. If I don't drink in order to please others or live up to their expectations, then I am falling in to the same trap I did as a child. I choose not to drink because I want to do that, not to get acceptance.

I am not saying "poor, poor, pitiful old me." I want to get the point across about how we, as a society, conditionally accept others on a regular basis, and we don't even realize it or the affect it has on others.

For me, the best way to justify my belief in unconditional acceptance is to look to my religion. I believe that we need to know that we are valuable because God made each and every one of us in his image. You can choose whatever rationale makes sense to you, but the end result should be this: Each of us is valuable as a person without having to do something good. This is how you need to think about ourselves if you want to have a healthy self-esteem.

Your thoughts and actions don't determine your value or worth. You are valuable because you exist. You don't need to have great thoughts or acquire many riches to be important. You are already valued, valuable, and important without those things.

Society focuses on what you do well, what you have, what you say, or how many scholastic degrees you have. This is living life with conditional acceptance. People say that you are a success and important because of your successes, and that you are not valuable if you do something bad. That is why most of us were brought up with conditional acceptance, because everybody else is doing it.

Important note: I am not referring to unconditional love; I am talking specifically about unconditional acceptance. All parents hopefully love their children. I am referring to not thinking that we need to do something well, or that we need to get an A on a test, or have a lot of money, or get an award to be valued, accepted or a considered a success.

Let me describe to you what I mean by a Dominant Parent Influence (DPI):

First let me give you an overriding concept:

"We can only relate in relation to the relationships we've known."

Your DPI (whether it is a parent, grandparent, guardian, older sibling, or whatever) was your first parental relationship that you knew. You then transfer that relationship (DPI) to other relationships you have. Know this:

<u>How your Dominant Parent Influence interacted with you is how you will interact with others.</u>

If you don't know that you are interacting with others as your DPI did with you, how can you change how you relate in your new relationships? It is almost impossible to do so.

If you think about it, you probably do things almost everyday because your parents or grandparents did it that way. Do you fold the blanket like your mom did? Do you do anything that is out of the ordinary because your family members did so? Do you get upset at the small things because your DPI did?

The diagram on the next page shows how you related to your DPI and how you transfer that relationship to others in life.

Let's say this image is you. The arrow pointing from you to the box labeled "DPI" is the relationship you had with your DPI as you were growing up. This relationship over the years has built either the healthy or an unhealthy self-esteem you have today. At a young age children learn a language they will be using for the rest of their lives (unless they become aware and consciously choose to change), and they have learned it primarily from their DPI.

The arrow from the box labeled "DPI" up to the box labeled "Authorities, Friends, Self" shows how you transfer your relationship with your DPI to other areas of your life.

From birth, you have related to your Dominant Parental Influence, and over the years that has become the way you relate to new relationships. You relate to authorities and friends like your DPI related to you. More importantly, you build your self-esteem on how your DPI, friends, and authorities have related to you and what they have said about you.

It boils down to this: Other people's thoughts and perspectives over the years have developed your self-esteem.

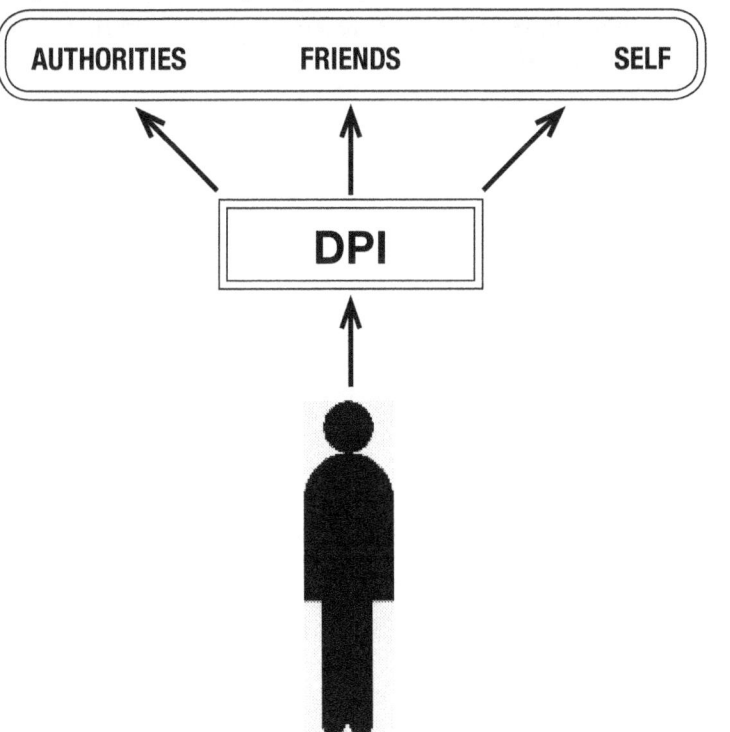

Figure 1.1 We can only relate in relation to the relationships we've known.

Special Points to ponder:

- Self-esteem is not self-esteem; it is DPI esteem.
- How your parents accepted you is how you accept others.
- You can only relate in relation to relationships you have known.
- Self-esteem is based upon past programming. It is not self-esteem; starting with your DPI, it is a reflection of other's perspectives about you.

So, who was your Dominant Parent Influence (DPI)?

Here are some questions you can ask yourself to determine who your DPI was:

- Who was the person you wanted to get attention from? You might have wanted to receive attention from this person, but didn't.
- Who did you want to impress?
- When you got a good grade, who did you want to notice it?
- Who was most influential in parenting you?

From these questions you can determine who your Dominant Parent Influence was. In turn, you can develop a healthy self-esteem by living life with unconditional acceptance. If you need to change your life from conditional to unconditional acceptance, you first need to know who your DPI was in order to change your course. Nothing can be changed without your first being aware of it or accepting it. Knowing who your DPI is allows you to focus on that person as your DPI and find if he or she raised you with conditional or unconditional acceptance.

So, were you raised with conditional acceptance like most people?

Here are some questions to ask yourself. Remember to focus on whoever your DPI was (or still is).

1. When you are (or were) punished, what is the main message surrounding the discipline?
2. When you do something poorly, what is the message you hear in your head?
3. When you do something well, what is the message you hear in your head?
4. What are three positive aspects about you?
5. What are three negative aspects about you?

Based on these questions, you should be able to find out if you where raised with conditional or unconditional acceptance. Your present answers can be traced back to when you were young. For example with the fifth bullet point above, if you heard things like 'I am dumb', or 'I can't do it', or 'they never pay attention to me', or 'I am not important,' this would mean you were most likely raised with conditional acceptance.

When you were disciplined, was it that you did a "bad" thing but you are still a valuable person? This is one way of knowing that you were raised with unconditional acceptance. Or was it that you "were bad." This is one way of showing that you were raised with conditional acceptance.

Do you hear positive or negative thoughts in your head?

If you hear more positive thoughts, it is more likely you where raised with unconditional acceptance because you have a healthy self-esteem. The thoughts you hear in your head are ones that your DPI said about you and what others have said about you.

However let me stress, that seeming to be self-confident while being arrogant is not a form of healthy self-esteem. It is actually a form of low self-esteem that shows serious insecurity. It may seem like a healthy one, but it seldom is. A person with a healthy self-esteem does not need to flaunt it by being arrogant.

Don't worry if you were raised with conditional instead of unconditional acceptance. There are three steps you can follow to live life with unconditional acceptance from this point on. Doing so produces a healthy self-esteem and will actually make many individuals around you happier, too.

Here are the three steps to having a healthy self-esteem:

1) Choose what standard of acceptance you want: Hopefully, you will choose unconditional acceptance and be flexible enough to accept other people unconditionally no matter what they do ... and to accept yourself in the same way.

2) Choose a new DPI role model who gives unconditional acceptance: Find a new DPI to follow. I personally use God as my leader in this, but you could use a grandparent, a friend, or a family member.

3) Treat everything as input. Listen to but don't react to others' criticism.

The first point is designed for you to decide which standard of acceptance you want to live life with. I hope it is unconditional acceptance, and I will trust that it is. I have learned that nothing can be changed unless we are first aware of it and accept it. It is amazing what a decision or choice can do for you mentally. Even if you don't like what you need to do, if you choose to do it, you will enjoy it more and you won't feel trapped.

The second point is so you can learn what it is like to live life with unconditional acceptance following a new DPI model, so in return you can live it. If your original DPI gave you unconditional acceptance (again, I'm not talking about unconditional love), you can learn and follow him or her. If not, then choosing a new DPI who does accept you unconditionally will give you a new model to learn from and follow.

You can give others unconditional acceptance even though others have given you conditional acceptance. When you do this, it is awesome and powerful for both of you.

The model I used for me personally was God. After I learned who my DPI was, I was able to apply the principle of God's unconditional acceptance in my life instead of my original DPI.

Living a life of unconditional acceptance, with a healthy self-esteem, will bring much peace and joy to your life.

A strong belief system, along with a healthy self-esteem, is vital. But there's more that needs to be established or developed and that is to develop a mind set of "Possibility Thinking." This means that you believe there is always a way to accomplish something you want to accomplish. Develop a perspective that always knows that there could be another possibility.

This is a concept and life principle that the Truby Achievement Center teaches. They say, "There's always a way!"

Third, develop a mind set of "Possibility Thinking"

Here is a story about knowing that there is always a way. When I was about 8 years old, I had trouble weighing enough to play football. There was a Pop Warner team, called the Napa Saints. (Some of you might have children who play in that league).

For you who don't know about this league, there are four different levels you can play on: junior peewees, peewees, junior midgets, and midgets. These divisions were determined by age and weight.

In my junior peewee year we were very good. We actually got all the way to the championship game. I can remember the week before our championship game. The game was 6 days away. To participate in the games, you had to be a certain age and a certain weight.

But, I had a problem coming into this game. I was of course the appropriate age, but I barely carried the necessary weight throughout the year. I was borderline throughout the year in weighing enough to be able to play. Because of the running I did in preparation for this championship game, I lost 8 pounds of body fat and water through my diet and sweat.

If I didn't weigh enough, I couldn't play in this championship game. I was worried and so were the coaches. I wanted to play so badly. Somehow I needed to weigh 7 more pounds to be able to play.

How was I going to do it?

In my life, I have always believed that there is always a way, to have the mind set called "Possibility Thinking." In each of our lives, we need to establish this mind set.

So, here is what it entails:

- You believe that you can do it, and
- You never think there is only one-way to accomplish something. More often than not, there is another way to do it. If what you are doing right now is not succeeding, you might need to make a change and try something else.

So, returning to the story: How can someone gain 7 pounds in less than a week? What would you do? I did it, but I hesitate to tell you how. My father helped me do something that was technically acceptable but a bit deceptive too. I'll tell you this funny story because the spirit of "possibility thinking" is there, but, now that I've grown up, I think I would do something differently.

In football, most players wear jock straps to protect themselves from getting hit. My father thought of designing a different kind of jock strap that would meet my need for protection and weight. He manufactured a jock strap with a metal plate for protection that just happened to weigh 7 pounds. That made me weigh just enough.

As I walked up to the scale, I had to walk bull-legged because that metal weight was hanging between my legs but it worked.

See, there is always a way. I weighed enough and I played. Everybody knew, even the men who weighed me, but I think that they thought it was great because I loved this game and really wanted to play.

You really shouldn't try to fix your problems with weights as we did. The point is to think with the mind set that there is always a way. So always be open and flexible to new possibilities.

One important ingredient in writing down effective goals is to make them realistic, but make them a stretch for you. I will get into more detail about this in the next chapter. In sports, for example, maybe you could train to be in a Senior Olympics or you could play flag football in a pick-up league in town.

It is vital to believe in yourself, and one way to do that is to build a healthy self-esteem. It is so powerful to develop the mind set of "possibility thinking," to have the perspective that there is always a way.

Another important ingredient in attaining your dreams is your attitude. So let's talk about your attitude now.

Fourth, why your attitude is so important.

What do you say when someone asks you how you are doing? If you mess up, what is your attitude like? When faced with a problem, do you respond positively or react negatively?

Your reaction to all of these questions depends upon what kind of attitude you have. A strong, positive attitude does not allow you to react in anger or worry. A good attitude does not allow you to run from problems; it allows you to confront them and overcome them.

A good attitude comes out in your presence and your actions. The presence of an individual who is strong and healthy gives the message of stability, strength, courage, and great leadership. We all need to have a winning attitude, especially when all odds are against us.

> "The biggest blessing is that a person can change his life by having a different attitude."
> — Curtis J. Steen

In crisis, do you strive to overcome or do you stop?

Your attitude needs to be focused on where you want to go. You can only accomplish what your attitude thinks you can. If you want to make a positive difference in people's lives, you have to have a positive, open attitude. If you have a negative attitude, you will probably stop when faced with obstacles and you will not have that positive effect you wanted to have.

The longer you live, the more you will realize the impact your attitude has on your life and other people's lives.

Attitude is more important than facts and positions. It is more important than the past, than education, than money, than circumstances, than failures, than successes, than what other people think, say, or do.

Attitude is more important than appearance, giftedness, or skill. It will make or break a company, a church, a home ... or you.

The remarkable thing is you have a choice every day regarding the attitude you will embrace every day. With other things you may not always have a choice. But with your attitude you do.

You cannot change your past. You cannot change the fact that people will act in a certain way. You cannot change the inevitable. The only thing you can do is play on the one string you have, and that is your attitude.

I have heard throughout my life from people whose opinions I respect highly that life is 10% what happens to me and 90% how I react to it.

It's the same for you. If you react well to a situation in life, you will have joy. But if you act negatively, you will feel defeated.

My attitude in elementary school was an attitude of defeat. They wanted to put me in special-ed, so I felt like I belonged there, and that was a negative attitude. My attitude was negative because I saw only negative things, like the fact that I couldn't read, or I couldn't write, and I couldn't speak clearly. That is how I saw myself and that is what I got … that is, until I chose to change my attitude.

Until I changed my attitude, my life stayed that way. When I changed my attitude after the 3rd grade, things changed in school. I was more positive and I saw the glass as being half-full and not as I looked at it before as half empty.

How did a change in attitude change my life? I am now the directing partner of a division of the Truby Achievement Center, called Soaring Eagles. I would like the young adults I coach to learn how to have a positive outlook. By having a positive attitude, they (and you) can create immediate change in their lives. I teach them the concept that they need to look at this world with a positive attitude and not a negative one.

There are many instances in life where you let circumstances control your attitude. Things like when it is raining for many days, or when your car breaks down on the side of the road, or if our flight is delayed. We get all boggled up and upset, bouncing off the walls in frustration because things that we have no control over are controlling our attitude.

> "Attitude is the window that you look through to see the world."
> — Curtis J. Steen

The only thing that you *can* control is your attitude and not the rain or the car that breaks down. What makes the difference in people is their attitude, maintaining a positive attitude in midst of crises as compared with a negative one.

So, develop an attitude that is positive and excitedly strive toward your goals even in stressful times.

What happens if you have a "bad" attitude?

It is never too late to change your attitude. If you slip and get upset, you can still change your attitude from negative to positive. When you have a good attitude, your problems seem less difficult to overcome. But if you have a negative attitude, a little problem will seem really big and overwhelming.

With the right attitude, all the problems in the world will not make you a failure. With the wrong mental attitude, all the help in the world will not make you a success. We all will fall into the gutter, but we need to be looking at the stars.

With a good, positive attitude, your obstacles look more like opportunities to succeed. It is not the end result that is life changing, it is the process and/or journey in getting there that is life changing.

A personal story

When I was young, I had a Nintendo game entertainment system. Do any of you have one? Or, do you know a friend who has one?

Well, I can remember when I was about 12 years old and my attitude went south a few times when I played my Nintendo. One time my friend and I were playing football against each other. I have loved football almost from the time I was born. I am also very competitive. That night we were playing and my attitude got bad, I mean really bad. I was mad at my friend for a week because he beat me on that video game. How sad is that?

When I lost, my attitude was seeing the glass half-empty. I should have been seeing it half-full and displayed a positive attitude.

A positive attitude will take you to a whole new level far beyond where knowledge, skills, and opinions can take you.

Many experts have said, "Your attitude will determine your altitude." If you have a positive attitude instead of a negative attitude, you will go to a whole new level.

We all need to develop an attitude of winning, an attitude of courtesy, an attitude of gratitude, and an attitude of kindness.

Lowell Peacock said, "Attitude is the first quality that marks a successful person. If a person has a positive attitude and is a positive thinker who likes challenges and difficult situations, then half of their success is achieved. On the other hand, if a person is a negative thinker who is narrow-minded and refuses to accept new ideas and has a defeatist attitude, they haven't got a chance."

When times get tough and you don't have a good attitude, you are doomed. If you have a positive attitude, anything is possible (backed up with action) because you have a positive attitude that likes challenges. A man or a woman can alter their lives by altering their attitudes. Attitude and thinking positively are important, but action behind a positive attitude and possibility thinking is the ultimate key.

Without action, a positive attitude is only good "Rah-Rah," with nothing behind it.

With the right attitude you can propel yourself to overcome obstacles, which will get you to your dreams.

So, how is your attitude today?

Last, know your "why."

Do you know your **why**? **Why** would you want that? **Why** do you want to accomplish something? **Why** do you wish to bring about change in your life?

In other words, what is your reason for wanting to accomplish something in your life?

Before I show you specifically how to set effective goals in the next chapter, I want you to understand the importance of knowing your *why*. It is vital to develop your ***why*** in conjunction with your what.

In finding your why, look to your heart and see if you really want what you are planning. If you write something down that you think you would like to have but don't really want it deep down inside, you will probably not accomplish it.

Don't only say that you want to be a firefighter because it is cool, but know the reason why you want to be a firefighter. Know what your heart says about firefighting.

It is so important to really understand why you choose what you choose. Don't just know the what, but know your why. The only way you will be effective in setting goals is to know your why. If you don't know your why, at the first or second struggle you will stop the process. You are more powerful and effective with a why.

Let's say you want to be a motivational speaker, or a counselor, or a mechanic, or maybe a teacher.

By asking yourself why you want to be a motivational speaker, counselor, a mechanic, or a teacher, you are getting to the core of your want.

I have found that when you get to the core of anything you can be successful. If you understand the core concepts of Mathematics, you will be able to do any equation, with a little guidance, because you understand the core concepts and you understand the why of the equation. When you are at the core, you will be unstoppable.

Also, when you find the why, the work involved will not be a bore, and perhaps it might make it fun and challenging. Additionally, it will not be fun without your why. The goal has to be meaningful for you or it will not come true.

The day I was able to understand my *why* for the Soaring Eagles Division for young adults was the day many things started to happen. More members came, bigger dreams popped-up, and a better attitude surfaced for me. I was happier with more success.

Also, when I got my why for this particular book, it developed very quickly. Your why comes from your heart and pushes you quickly to your goals because obstacles and struggles have less influence when your heart is involved.

Living life by choice

We all need to live life by choice. If you can learn to choose what you are doing and not say, "I *have* to do it," it will make your life more fulfilled and happier. We all have the freedom to choose, which means we all have the freedom to choose what we want to do and what we want to be. It is important to choose what you want and not what anybody else wants for you. It is *your* life, not your next-door neighbor's. Personally, I have asked God to be in control of my life and what I do, but I choose with Him what I want.

Knowing your why will develop strengths in many other areas of your life, strengths like ambition, faith, hope, persistence, and drive. The why will keep you going towards your goals. Your goals and the efforts to achieve them will be enjoyable. Knowing your why will build a desire to achieve what you want.

Do you have your why?

Chapter 2

"With chapter one's mind set …
… sit down and plan your direction."

In this chapter you will learn:
- The importance of planning;
- How to find your life purpose;
- The importance of writing down your dreams;
- How to set effective goals;
- The importance of being flexible.

"Why do I have to plan? Do I really need to? I don't have the time. I'm too busy. And by the way, I have it all up here in my head, anyway."

I respond to that attitude with a decisive, "No, this is not good." It is very smart to plan your life and I will prove to you why.

Big businesses make plans to be successful. People develop business plans every day, but why can't they do it for their own lives?

Are they saying that their life is not important? Of course it is important.

Trust me, you will always do better and be more effective in getting what you want when you plan. The time you will spend planning will save more time in the future. Nobody would fund you if you wanted to start a business without a business plan. In planning, what you are doing is developing a road map to get to your destination quicker, easier, and more efficiently.

Just think if you were driving in San Francisco, California to a restaurant you'd never been to, and you didn't bring directions. San Francisco is a very busy place.

Wouldn't that be a waste of time? Of course, you will waste more time driving around trying to find the restaurant than if you brought a map or someone who had been there.

It sounds pretty dumb not to plan, but there are many people who do not plan their lives. They don't plan the lives they want, so they keep working hard going in circles because they have no clear direction.

That's how people can get lost in a cornfield and never get out—going in circles, just like people working hard with no written plan.

Here is another reason to plan your life.

I am not sure where I heard these statistics, but they seem so true to life. There are 3% of those in the world who are rich, and 3% of those in the world who write down their goals. Likewise, only 1% of the world is wealthy and 1% who write down their goals with a due date. This seems to make sense. When you plan and write down that plan, you do better. Little things always make the difference.

Why are such a small percentage of people financially successful?

I believe there are only two things that differentiate those who are successful in life from those who are not. One is that they write down their goals, and the second is that the ones who do write down their goals never stop believing in themselves. They keep persisting no matter what gets in their way.

Five reasons why planning is essential

1) You get to your destination quicker and easier.
2) You are more focused.
3) You don't live life on inertia.
4) You are more efficient.
5) You have direction.

By planning and by knowing what you want to do before you do it, accomplishing your goals becomes more of a breeze for you. That is why people strategize and plan before they open a new company. They develop a business plan to be successful. Contractors have the dimensions already in place before they build, and good restaurant owners know what food they will serve before they open up for business.

Doesn't this seem to be "Duh? Of course."

So, why do many people not plan their life? It comes down to a lack of discipline and not truly understanding the benefit of planning.

Do your goals need adjustment?

After someone realizes the importance of planning, he also needs to realize that there will be times when the plan needs to be changed in the middle of the course.

Sometimes when people have a plan, they think they have to stay with that plan forever and not allow for changes. This can cause bigger problems and less efficient outcomes because it makes a person feel trapped. Or a person just has done it that way for so long and they keep on doing it, even if there is an easier way to do it. I will discuss determining when it's a good time to make a change in Chapter 3.

But for now, I will say this. Sometimes things do not go your way and you need to make changes and be flexible in making those changes. The contractor might have built the window frame too small and now he or she might have to put in a smaller window because of the mistake or change in dimensions. But the goal of completing the house remains the same.

Do you live life on inertia?

Throughout my life many people have guided and given me the insight not to live life on inertia. Network 21, the Truby Achievement Center, and other mentors of mine have taught me about how living life on inertia can interfere with my goals.

Living life on inertia means you keep on doing what you have done simply because you've always done it that way. If you want things different in your life, then living life on inertia is not your answer. If you are living life on inertia—doing the same things over and over yet expecting different results—you will not see the results you want.

Some people say the definition of insanity is keeping on doing what you've always done and expecting different results. This is parallel to living life on inertia, doing the same things over and over.

If you are living life on inertia, you will keep on living that way unless you consciously choose to change your course of action. And you can change ... if you want to.

Know this, nothing can be changed or improved without your first becoming aware of it and *really wanting it to change.*

If you are living life on inertia and you want to change, you first need to make a conscious decision to switch your course of direction.

So, how do you do that exactly?

Make a change in your actions by concentrating, thinking, and doing the exercises in this chapter. Don't just do them; do them with heart and drive and passion.

> "If you don't know where you are going, how will you know when you get there?"
> — Anonymous

By doing these exercises, you will then live life everyday focused on your new direction and not on inertia.

In Chapter 1, I stressed the importance of believing, knowing your "why", having a healthy self-esteem, and having the mind set of "Possibility Thinking." You first need to have these ingredients in place before you start to plan your future; you can think of them as making up your backbone.

When you combine all the necessary ingredients discussed in Chapter 1 with a plan, you *will* be powerful and productive.

Living life on inertia is not a way for you to live life anymore. You need to be so pumped and ready to go in life, you won't want to sit down. The right lottery numbers are not the only means to become financially independent; if you follow these steps and refuse to live life on inertia, you will make yourself successful in business.

Here is a basic principle. If you keep on persisting, with prayer, you will create more momentum and more options, and successes will come from that momentum you created. More things will pop up and flash before your eyes when you keep on going. The more work you do, the more opportunities come to your doorstep.

By planning, you will reach your destination quicker and more easily because you will be focused on your target. You will be able to be more productive, live life more fulfilled, and be more successful.

The first step in planning is finding your life purpose. You begin with the end point or overriding purpose in mind, and then you look at dreams, then step back again and set effective goals to make your life purpose and dreams a reality.

Finding your life purpose

How do you find your life purpose?

Well, this is how I found mine. I am an individual who prays about everything, and when I pray I get goose bumps. I receive goose bumps because God makes me feel good inside. Remember the seminar I attended in San Diego, California? Well, it was so influential that I got goose bumps just like the Lord gives to me when I pray. I thought that if a seminar can give me goose bumps like the Lord does, then I know that is where God wants my heart to be.

So I found my life purpose at that seminar, which is to make a positive difference in people's lives. When I saw those speakers influencing others up on that stage, I knew that was what I wanted to do.

When I see someone grow and become better, I receive the gift of goose bumps. This sounds dumb, goose bumps, but I know God is using me for His benefit when I influence someone positively.

So, what gives you goose bumps? I don't mean when you are cold. *I mean when you are truly inspired.*

This might help you find your purpose. But first let me give you some background on what a life purpose is. This information about what your life purpose is and how to find it is from personal experience.

> "Look to find your vision and life purpose, and they will find you."
> — Curtis Steen

Most all life purposes consist of two ingredients:

- Others centered
- Service oriented

My life purpose is to make a positive difference in people's lives.

A true life purpose has the two components listed above. My life purpose is others-centered because I want to help others. It is service oriented because I am giving the services of motivation, training, tools, and support taught within my Soaring Eagles Division.

My main purpose in writing this book is to help others turn their dreams into today's reality—to help you turn your life's dreams into your reality. To turn your dreams into today's reality, you first begin with the end in mind. So, what do you want your life purpose to be; what do you want to bring to the table?

Teresa is an amazing woman who has a different life purpose from mine. It is to help people see new possibilities in leadership, in connection, and in seeing new ideas. She has a passion for teaching people how to see all possibilities. Her life purpose has the two ingredients above. It is others centered, and it is service-centered in teaching people how to see new possibilities. This is her life purpose, but it does not have to be yours. The main point is for *you* to choose what you want your life purpose to be. There is not a right or wrong or better or worse life purpose; it is just what you want and *that* is what is important.

Do you know yours yet? If not, here is some more help.

Think about where your heart is. What makes you want to get out of bed in the morning? What gives you goose bumps? Why are you here? *What would you do for free?*

Think about what you want to be. I don't mean charismatic, energetic, or those similar things. I mean how do you want to serve others on earth?

Let's say you are thinking about what you want to do, but you don't know exactly what it is. You might want to be a mechanic, or a consultant, or an electrician, or a carpenter, or maybe a fire fighter, or a police officer, or an engineer.

How do you figure out which one you want to be?

First, you can list the benefits of each, and if you know your life purpose, you can ask the question: "Does it fit your life purpose?"

But, which one of these gives you goose bumps, which one do you think you will have the most fun doing, which one would you do for free? You know you want to help others and all of these occupations do help others in one way or another. But how do you really want to help others? Let's say you decide that you want to be a firefighter.

As a firefighter what could be your life purpose?

Well, what you do is to think about the overall idea of what you want, that is, to be a firefighter. Think specifically about how it can help others and how it serves others.

A firefighter serves others by protecting them. And of course it is helping others by saving lives. A possible life purpose is this: You are really here to help others and protect them from danger. Basically your life purpose consists of an overall idea of what you want to be in life. Is that what you really want? Does that give you goose bumps? If it does, then do it. But let's say you want to help people and protect them, but you really don't want to be a firefighter.

What, then, are some other career paths that involve helping others and protecting them? You could go through the same thought process and ask the same kind of questions about the carpenter, or an engineer, or a police officer. Keep on doing that with each one and see what you really, truly like.

A police officer and an environmental engineer protect us and help others. So what you need to do is make a decision on what you want to do in actual work that encompasses your life purpose. Does it encompass what you love? When it does, you will live life more fulfilled and happy.

Let's say at this time you are a firefighter, but later on you change your mind. You want to do something different. You will still be happy and more fulfilled when you do something that encompasses your life purpose.

You just need to find something that encompasses your life purpose of protecting people and/or protecting the environment if that is your purpose. You could switch from a being firefighter to an environmental engineer and still live out your life purpose. How is this? It is because you will still be protecting the environment but in a different career and in different circumstances.

Have you found your life purpose? If you have a life purpose, that's great. If you don't have one yet, no problem. Keep on thinking and jot down your life purpose in the area provided below. For some people it takes many years to find it. It personally took me 3 years to find and realize my true life purpose.

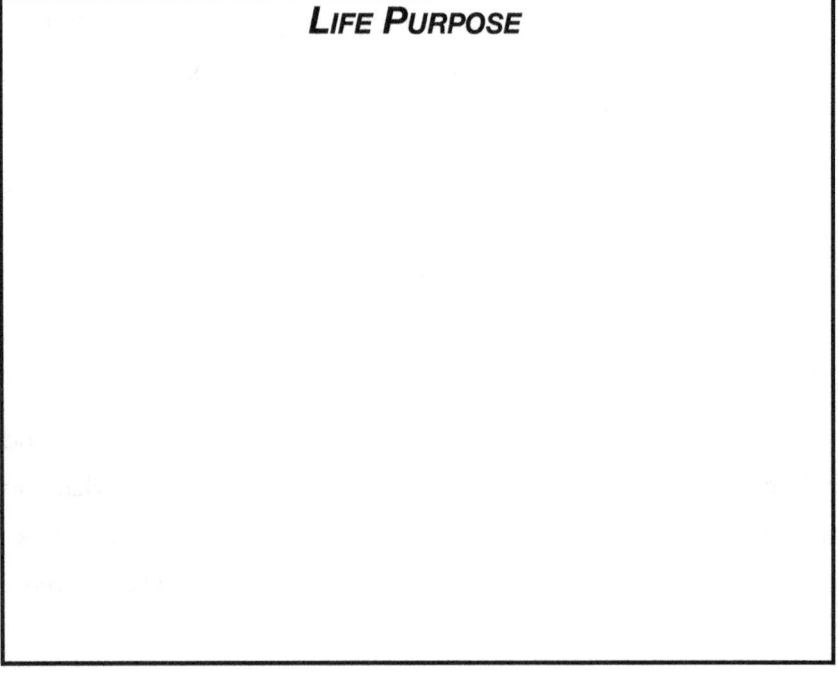

Writing down your dreams

Imagine for a moment about one particular student in a classroom of seventeen. These students were in 3rd grade and were asked to create a life dream. They were asked to paint a picture on a big piece of paper of what they wanted in life of what they wanted to be and have in the future.

All of the students received an "A" except for one student who received a "D."

> *"Your life is a blank wall. Pick up the pen, and start writing what you want."*
> — Curtis J. Steen

This student went to the teacher and asked why he received a "D" on this paper. She replied, "This is an unrealistic dream. Your family is poor and unsuccessful. It is an unrealistic dream for you." Then she said, "If you redo this paper I will reevaluate your grade."

He went home and thought about it long and hard, even asked for guidance from his parents. His parents said, "This one is up to you. It is your dream and your life. You need to make this decision if you want to redo it or not."

He sat in his room all night, praying and thinking. On that piece of paper he had drawn a huge white house that had big windows in front and a pool in the back with a 5-acre ranch around the house. He had 6 horses and 5 cows. There was a barn in back of the house, along with a big patio, where they had their family gatherings.

He went into the class the next morning and walked up to the teacher and said here is my project. She smiled as she grabbed it but stopped smiling when she looked at it.

She replied, "Your picture is the same. You didn't change anything."

He then said, "I will keep my dream and you can keep your grade."

My 3rd grade teacher said that I was not smart enough and I would never graduate from college. It hurt when she said it, but I proved her wrong. I graduated from U.C. Davis in June of 2000. The power of your dreams and what you want can be so moving. This young person didn't let someone steal his dream. Don't let anyone steal yours.

> "If you talk more about your past than your future, and it is more exciting, your mind set is a has been."
>
> — Curtis J. Steen

What you think is what you will get.

What you think is what you will get, I promise. Whatever you focus on consistently is what you will receive in life.

You get what you order and expect in life. If you order big, positive stuff, you get big and better stuff. But if you order bad stuff, that is what you will get. Writing down your dreams is about seeing your vision for the future.

This part of achieving your goals is *the most* exciting and most liberating experience you can have. You are thinking what you want to do in the future because you can.

It is liberating to dream the biggest dreams. It is healthy to dream and get yourself pumped up about the future and what you can do. But it is also necessary to be realistic in your dreams.

So, how do you dream?

First, don't let yourself say that you can't achieve your dream when you start to write. What helped me was writing down one hundred things that I wanted to do, have, and be. After I finished writing, I looked them over and started to plan what I *really* wanted. (I chose the number one hundred for no particular reason. You can do more or less. It is up to you).

The reason I am asking you to write down some dreams by brainstorming is for you to get your mind to start thinking about new possibilities of wants.

Based on my own experience and other's experiences, I have found your future will be whatever you mentally picture it to be. And you can't have a picture unless you first start to dream.

When writing down your dreams for your life, start by looking 5 to 10 years out. If you are in your 20s, I don't recommend looking to when you turn 50 because envisioning turning 50 years old is harder than seeing yourself as 30 years old. Think about a shorter period of time. It makes more sense and you can grasp it by looking to age 25 or so. If you are 50 years old, look to when you are 55 or so, not 90.

Use an additional piece of paper for your brainstorming; there is not enough room in this book to allow for that. Your dreams must be bigger than can be contained on this page.

Some observations about brainstorming.

First, you will find out that your most moving and exciting dreams will encompass your life purpose. And …

Second, you will be able to turn some of your dreams into effective goals that you can accomplish, goals that are manifested within your life purpose. Okay, start writing your dreams about your life purpose now. When you are done, come back to this place in the book.

Here is how you get more focused.

Look at all the dreams you wrote down on paper and decide which ones are most important to you now. Choose seven dreams at a time. After you accomplish these seven, add new ones. I provided a space below for you to write down your seven most important dreams.

Write down seven dreams (long-term goals), ones that you will accomplish 5 to 10 years from now ...

1. _____

_____

2. _____

_____

3. _____

_____

4. _____

_____

5. _____

_____

6. _____

_____

7. _____

_____

I recommended that you only focus on 7 dreams at a time. Why do I say this?

You can easily get overwhelmed when you try to focus on too much. You will then be less effective in achieving your dreams.

As you finish or accomplish a dream, add another one to the list. Or, if you prefer, wait until you have completed most of them and then write more dreams down from your big brainstorming list.

I wrote 100 dreams a number of years ago that I am still working on accomplishing today. I keep on accomplishing them, and I keep on bringing in new ones.

How do you translate your dreams into today's reality?

Well, here is how you master that challenge. Many people write down some dreams but don't go any further. This next step is where many fail. They do not set their goals properly. Many people do not know how to write effective goals.

Writing effective goals

How do you write effective goals so you can achieve them more effectively?

Goals are like steppingstones, little steppingstones. Having these small steps is where success comes from. Consistent little steps will get you to your overall dreams.

Have you ever heard it said that it is the little things that make a difference? Of course you have … and that is true.

Many of my mentors have said, "Small things are of greater value than big things. Could an ocean exist without each drop?"

My mentors were right on. That is exactly how you need to look at your goals. You need to look at them like they are the steppingstones in getting what you want, in achieving your dreams. It's the day-in/day-out activities that build empires. It was the day-in/day-out work ethic that allowed me to publish this book. It is the day-in/day-out work ethic that will carry you to your goals.

Before I show you specifically how to set effective goals for increased accomplishment, here is brief overview why you need goals and why you benefit from setting them.

> *"You won't get everything you want, but you will never get anything you first don't want."*
> — *Anonymous*

With goals, it takes less time ...

The shortest distance between two points is a straight line. Think of goals as your straight line. Look at the diagrams below and on the next page: with and without small stepping stone goals along the way.

The diagram below is a straight line. It is your *idealized* path to accomplish your dreams. "A" is where you are now, and "B" is your dream, your end point.

Figure 2.1 The idealized path to a dream — It never happens this way

But, in life the reality is that you will have struggles and bends in the road. The diagram on the next page illustrates your path **without** the steppingstones goal. Huge turns and bends. There way involves far more time and effort. And with all of those twists, turns, bends and backslides, you might never get to the endpoint: your dream. Pursuit of a dream without goals to get there is a rocky road.

Figure 2.2 Your path to a dream without steppingstone goals along the way. It can be a very rough road, indeed.

And, finally, the illustration below shows what happens to our path with small stepping stone goals along the way. You take less time and spend less effort for the same outcome because your small steps keep pulling you back toward the direct, idealized (but unrealistic) path.

Figure 2.3 Your path to a dream with steppingstone goals to smooth out your path. It's not perfect, but it is so much easier than without these goals.

Goals are easier and attained more quickly without big bumps in the road. With short term, stepping stone goals, your turns or roadblocks will not be as wavy. Life will always bring struggles and challenges, and I will show you how to overcome them in Chapter 6.

Setting effective goals ...

Now I will show you specifically how to set effective goals that create increased success.

There are five key elements in setting effective goals ...

Key Element #1: Write down your goals.

This is an easy one. Simply take five minutes and write down what you think your goals are to accomplish your dreams on the other page.

Why is it important to do this? Not doing this is the one most important factors that holds people back from achieving their goals. This step is so simple yet so powerful ... and unfortunately it is so easily overlooked.

Writing down your goals helps you keep focused on them because you can keep looking at them and constantly thinking about them. Many people think they don't need to do this, but trust me, if they did it, they would succeed more often and more quickly.

I recommend setting both hard and easy goals. Set easy goals for the purpose of building your success path and your belief, and set hard goals for the purpose of stretching yourself to attain more difficult dreams and to push yourself to higher grounds. Doing so produces a good work ethic.

Many experts have said that people who write goals down and periodically review them are more successful at attaining their goals than people who just think about them.

So write down your goals. I will provide a space after point #5 so you can write down your personal goals to acquire your dreams.

Key Element #2: Make your goals measurable

You need to make your goals measurable. For example, let's say you want to save $5,000 in one year. What will you need to save to do this? You will need to save roughly $14 per day to reach $5,000 in one year. This is very easily measured by looking in your bank account and seeing a $14 deposit every day. If you only saved $10 one day, you have not accomplished your goal for that day. You accomplished a partial amount but not the full amount. You can save more the next day to keep on track.

The point is this, you can measure your goal. If you can't measure it, it is not a goal.

Let's say your goal is you want to graduate from college? You can measure that at graduation. You set a goal of receiving an A, B, or a C on all your grades throughout high school and college. This is easily measured because the teacher or professor gives you your grade at the end of each semester or quarter. You know if you got an A, B, or C.

Things like integrity, charisma, and determination are harder to measure. If you want to choose those, you will have to find an indirect way to measure them. Here is how I did it. I measured them by the amount of books I read and how many tapes I listened to on these subjects.

But the main point is to make your goals measurable.

Key Element #3: Determine a "by when" (a due date)

When do you want your goal accomplished? What is your approximate or designated time to achieve it? When do you need it done?

It is really important that you do this. Researchers have found that 3% of people write down their goals, and 1% write down their goals with due dates. Interestingly, there are 3% wealthy and 1% rich people in the United States. Is writing down goals a factor in these people's financial success? I really believe it is.

I am convinced that some people are rich because they write down their goals appropriately with due dates, because of their belief systems, and because they focus on their target in ways that are effective.

When I was 19 years old I saw a Harley Davidson that captured my attention. It was so beautiful and shiny, so powerful … and so tempting. I decided I wanted to get one.

Here was my process in how I sought to get it. If I saved $10 per day for the next four years, I would have at least, not including interest, $14,400 in my savings account. I then could buy the Harley that I wanted, and that is exactly what I did. I got the Harley when I was 23 years old, 4 years right on my due date. I was able to accomplish my goal by the due date I set. If I hadn't set a due date, I know I would still be wanting—and not riding—my Harley today.

So, whatever you want in life, determine a "by when" date that you want or need it. Some people might think this is forcing you to do something, and in a very powerful way it is. But in Chapter 1 I spoke about making sure you want what you choose. If you really want it, then setting a due date will keep you on track to accomplish it.

Key Element #4: Write your goal in positive affirmation, present tense form.

Let me share with you what I mean by this.

There is a difference between saying I weigh 180 pounds and need to lose 30 pounds, and saying I weigh 150 pounds with 30 extra pounds.

What is the difference? The difference is that one is in a positive affirmation, present tense form, and one is not. Saying I am 150 pounds with 30 extra pounds is a positive affirmation, present tense, form.

What you say is what you will get. And if you say you are 180 pounds you will become what you already weigh, 180 pounds. You won't get to 150. What you focus on in life is what you will get out of life.

While you are 180 pounds, you tell yourself that you are a 150-pound person because that is your goal, and in doing this you are preparing your mind to be 150 pounds. Whatever you think is what you will get. This is in fact a different mind set and not a simple mind game. I have never known someone who thought they were overweight, who kept on saying that they were overweight, who actually lost weight long term. Have you? And I have never known a person who thought that they couldn't achieve something and achieved it. When you state things positively, you are setting yourself up for success, which creates actions, which creates accomplishment.

What do I mean by being positive?

All that I mean is to make your goal statement positive. Don't be negative ... because what you think is what you will get. Try to always think on the positive side of things.

What do I mean by writing your goals in the present tense, positive affirmation form?

What I mean is to write down your goals like you have already accomplished it. Write down your goals saying, "I am charismatic. I have published ten books. I am buying the house of my dreams." Do it in the present tense.

Key Element #5: Make your goals realistic, but make them a "stretch."

When you write your goals, make sure they are realistic. This was the biggest and most influential factor for me in accomplishing my goals in life.

When I was young, I dreamed the biggest dreams imaginable but I ended coming up short. I dreamed too big, which made me not succeed and ended up putting more stress on me. It was like I wanted to build a house on the moon when I first should have put a house on top of a mountain.

Dreaming big dreams is fine, but you need to evaluate where you are in life and see if it is realistic. But remember to stretch yourself where you have not gone before. The house I wanted to buy was not realistic five years ago, but it is today.

I can remember saying when I was 15 that I was going to be financially independent by the time I was 25. This was somewhat accomplishable. I could have done it by winning the lottery or inheriting a lot of money. But the time frame was unrealistic. It was too much of a stretch. Most 25-year olds are not financially independent.

What did I really mean by being financially independent? I meant not having to work for somebody else. To go where I wanted to go and to do everyday what I wanted to do. This was a great dream, but I actually made it too big. It stressed me out so I wasn't effective in working to accomplish it … or anything else for that matter. There are ways that this goal could be accomplished, but in my life I was not ready. If I would have said I wanted to be financially independent by the age of 35, and had developed a plan to accomplish it, the goal would have been more realistic, and it also would be a big stretch—but one that is more realistic and more likely to be accomplished. I am 26 years old now, and I am still dreaming big. But now the difference in my success is that I set effective, more realistic goals

Another thing I do is to focus on the smaller dreams first and bigger dreams next. I set goals more realistically by having the little goals—steppingstones—to get me to the big goals.

In the past I would say things like I want to buy a house in a year. I should have said I needed to save $100 per day for four years. Then I can afford the type of house I had my eye on. Instead of thinking of making $600,000 per year, first think about making $2,000 per month, and then $10,000 per month, and so on.

I shared with you before that I wanted a house and getting it has taken much longer than I expected it would take. For a time, I got down on myself. But today I have developed a plan, which includes steppingstones in getting to my dream. I am actually getting there faster with the little things than in trying to think about the big things, because I am more efficient and happier. I am able to work faster and smarter with this attitude and perspective.

Creating smaller goals makes it easier to accomplish your tasks. The success you create will develop a higher morale and a stronger belief along with promoting a healthy self-esteem. Can you see how this builds? When you set smart, step-by-step goals, you realize the big goals.

When you step up to the plate and your first try is a huge goal, it is unlikely you will succeed. You will get down on yourself and actually hinder yourself more. I call this the double whammy, because when this happens, you won't want to accomplish *anything else.* Your positive actions will stop because you lack belief or motivation.

But on the other hand, make sure to stretch yourself. This is very important. People do better and learn more when they are challenged. Think about it. When you get into a routine and do the same things over and over again, do you feel pumped up for the future and motivated to do things? Do you feel challenged? Most likely you would agree with me when I say, "Probably not."

Here is a fun analogy: think of us humans as rubber bands. If you let a rubber band go without stretching it, it will just fall, but if you stretch the rubber band and let it go, it will fly and have momentum, movement, and, potentially, growth.

Think about your life. Have you said something similar to "I want to be challenged more at work? I want something new to do. With something different, I would work harder."

I understand those who believe in the Lord might have difficulty in determining if something is realistic or not because with the Lord anything is possible. But …

As I shared with you earlier, you need to develop the mind set of possibility thinking. To believe that there is "always a way." I personally believe this because I have given the Lord control of my life and through him anything *is* possible.

So what is realistic?

What can be impossible to mankind is possible through the Lord. So you need to decide what is realistic for you *on earth* and let the Lord take you to the next level. Have faith in the Lord that he will provide your personal wants, and leave the rest to him. *Sometimes* you ask for things, but they do not come true because the Lord has an even better plan.

Lets review the five key elements to setting goals

1) Write your goals down;
2) Make them measurable;
3) Determine a "by when" or due date;
4) Write them in a positive affirmation, present tense form, and
5) Make them realistic, but make them a stretch.

Stick very closely to these and I promise that your odds of success will increase tremendously.

Here is a question to ask yourself to know if you have set a measurable goal or not:

When you reach your goal will you know, for certain, that you have accomplished your goal? If you can't know for certain it is *not* a clear goal.

For fun, here are some of my goals:

1) By June 1, 2005, I am influencing 1500 Soaring Eagle members for the better.
2) I am reading 15 minutes every day in a motivational or leadership book.
3) I have written 20 motivational and leadership books by the age 48.
4) I am saving $1,500 every month in the year 2004.

So, now you try it … Write down effective goals to accomplish the dreams you have listed above. Write down each of your dreams below, and for each dream write down effective goals to help you realize that dream. (I provided space for five goals for each dream. You might need more or fewer goals. Life example: I wanted to purchase a Harley. To get the Harley, I only needed to accomplish one goal.)

Dream #1: _____

_____

_____

_____

Goal: _____

_____

Goal: _____

_____

Goal: _____

_____

Goal: _____

_____

Goal: _____

_____

Dream #2: _____

_____

_____

Goal: _____

_____

Goal: _____

_____

Goal: _____

_____

Goal: _____

_____

Goal: _____

_____

Anything's Possible! Chapter 2

Dream #3: _____

_____

_____

Goal: _____

Goal: _____

Goal: _____

Goal: _____

Goal: _____

_____

Dream #4: _____

_____

_____

Goal: _____

Goal: _____

Goal: _____

Goal: _____

Goal: _____

_____

Dream #5: _____

_____

_____

Goal: _____

_____

Goal: _____

_____

Goal: _____

_____

Goal: _____

_____

Goal: _____

_____

Dream #6: _____

_____

_____

Goal: _____

_____

Goal: _____

_____

Goal: _____

_____

Goal: _____

_____

Goal: _____

_____

Dream #7: _____

_____

_____

_____

Goal: _____

Goal: _____

_____

Goal: _____

_____

Goal: _____

_____

Goal: _____

_____

Sit Down & Plan Your Direction

Again, I have left space for only seven dreams so that you will not be overwhelmed. But I have left ample space for the stepping stone goals that will get you there. Personally, when I was shooting for too many dreams, I became overwhelmed, and I ended up not accomplishing anything.

It is like if you play sports, a team only wants you to play one sport at a time because your focus goes off of one to the other, taking you away from complete focus and strength building. In college, I wanted to play soccer while I was playing football, but the football coach urged me not to.

Setting goals based upon your dreams builds hope for the future. It creates a spirit of wanting to be a better person.

So let's do it. Go accomplish your dreams and goals, but remember to be flexible!

Chapter 3

"Keep focused ...

    ... and revisit your plan daily."

In this chapter, you will learn the importance of:
- Reviewing your goals on a regular basis;
- Keeping focused on your target;
- Adjusting your dreams appropriately;
- Taking everything along the way as "input;"
- Persisting, persevering, and persisting some more.

    Do *you* review your goals? Do you look them carefully over on a regular, ongoing basis?

    Reviewing your goals on a consistent basis is powerful. I have found that by studying your goals on a regular basis, you stay focused.

Try to review your goals in the morning, at lunch, and lastly before going to bed <u>every day</u>. This helps keep your mind focused on your target. Remember, whatever you think about *is* what you will get. Reviewing your goals three times every day helps build focus on what you want and internalizes it for you. In return, your goals will seem easier and more attainable.

> "If you get kicked off your race track, get back on course."
> — Curtis J. Steen

If you are only able to review your goals once a day, I would recommend you do it before you go to sleep, because your subconscious mind is at work at that time. When you get into your subconscious, it gives you the belief that you "can." Your subconscious mind doesn't really know the difference between reality and fantasy. So if you say, "I am a millionaire" when you are not, your subconscious mind doesn't realize that it is not true, and it will dream about it. This in turn can help you get to your target with the belief factor. It is as if you have already done it, so you can do it again. The subconscious mind is powerful, and you need to remember this. Whatever goes in comes out, and at the same time, whatever goes in stays in.

Keeping focused on your target or goal

How do you keep focused on your target? Let me use myself as an example.

Recently I have been playing a lot of basketball. I am not a good basketball player, but I love the sport. I have been playing more basketball than I ever had and it has been a good learning experience. Lately, my shooting has been getting better. Why?

Keep Focused ... And Revisit Your Plan Daily

Well, I applied what I was teaching about how focus is important. In this case, it was important for me to focus on the basketball hoop.

Basketball players can relate to the importance of focusing on the hoop while shooting. Since I have been focusing on the hoop in this fashion, my shot has gotten better. I have been making double the shots because of focus.

Here is a story about my football days. I played college football at U.C. Davis as a receiver and punt returner. Being a receiver and a punt returner, I needed to have great focus.

When the quarterback throws the ball, it comes with great velocity. A receiver has to get his hands out, away from his body, and concentrate or he won't catch the ball. If the receiver tries to catch it with his body, it will either hurt or it will bounce off. So, in order to catch a football, the receiver must have great focus and concentration.

Punt returning is also a time for focus. There was a time when I was back deep, ready for the other team to punt. I remember that the punter got all of it, and kicked it over my head.

I started running backward to catch the ball. The complexity of the situation required more concentration and focus than the average punt. When someone runs, they need more focus than if they are standing still. So in this case, I was running back and looking over my shoulder. But, as the ball went through the air it was not in a spiral, it was flying end over end. So as I was running back, looking over my shoulder for the ball, it was moving dramatically back and forth in the air. There was also about a 15-mile per hour wind, which didn't help the situation at all.

Focus was vital at this moment. This was the hardest punt I ever had to catch. Pressure was on me because it was the fourth quarter with 2 minutes left and we were down by a field goal. All of these problems were riding on the ball as it came down toward me.

But, I kept focused and I caught that ball and actually had a pretty good punt return that gave our team good field position. In the end, we won.

Ryan, my brother, and Clifford, my father, helped me develop focus. My brother was amazing with punt returns and gave me his secrets. To improve my concentration, my father would throw tennis balls as high as he could up in the air and I would practice catching them. I started practicing this type of focus when I was 8 years old. The balls went so high that they would disappear.

These sports examples are true in all aspects life not just in sports. You need focus in business and in work. If you want to do a good job, or accomplish your goals, the dynamics of being focused do not change whether you are a surgeon, a mill worker, a millionaire in the making, or a college punt returner.

Reviewing your goals on a regular basis is an important way to keep you focused on your destination.

If needed, adjust your dreams

When you review your goals three times daily, you are able to keep focused, but you are also able to adjust your dreams and goals when

Keep Focused ... And Revisit Your Plan Daily

needed. If you need to make changes, additions, or deletions, you can. Reviewing your goals has two main purposes:

1) To keep yourself focused, and

2) To adjust your dreams.

When you set your goals, you need to be specific about them in order to accomplish them. But that does not mean you cannot adjust them to make them more realistically achievable. For instance, you may have found a better course of action with a more realistic time line.

But if you adjust your dream, only do it if it will result in a *positive change*. Don't change your dream because you are lazy, tired, discouraged, or think you can't do it. It is not an option to keep on changing your dreams because you think you can't do it.

It is OK to make your dreams bigger or smaller in order to be more realistic about accomplishing them, but the key is to adjust them <u>so you can be effective in your life</u>.

I personally had to change my time frame, or due date, when I wanted to buy a house. It was taking longer than expected, so I just needed to change the time frame, not any of the other four points in setting effective goals.

The need to adjust makes you feel free in your decisions, thus less forced and tied down. Your main focus needs to be on being effective in accomplishing what you want.

But remember, it is self-defeating if you make adjustments as justification for abandoning your dreams. Don't let that happen. Use this point in adjusting your dreams and goals as a way for you to be more effective, not for an easy excuse to abandon your dream.

You might think some of your dreams and goals are attainable in the next 4 months, but they really are attainable in 9 months. It is all right to change the time frame if you have examined the situation *honestly*, so be flexible and allow for change.

Take everything along the way as input ...

If you make a mistake, learn from it. Know this: It is all right if you make a mistake. If you do well, learn from your success as well. But regardless of whether an occurrence is positive or negative, take everything along the way as input and become better from your life experiences.

> "We can all have a new beginning. When we fail, it is not the falling down but the staying down that hurts us."
> — Curtis J. Steen

In Chapter 6, I will help you overcome obstacles in your way. You need to learn how to overcome these obstacles because they are simply not going to go away. As you have undoubtedly noticed, life does not always go the way you want or hope. One way to overcome and be positive when something is not going the way you hoped is to take it in as *input*. A good mind set to have is this: Always learn from what you have done well and always learn from what you have done poorly ... replicate the good or improve because of the bad. But get better because of it all.

Let's say you want to drive from California to Maine in your car. You think about starting to drive that long way from California to Maine and you jump into your seat with enthusiasm. In life our goals seem to be a long way away just as Maine does if you are starting to drive there. But you are pumped about the future in what you can accomplish. This is like when you jump into a new business, job, or idea. You are excited, but in all likelihood, you are not looking forward to the long drive or the work involved in getting there.

You turn the key, turning your engine on, just like how you believe in your pursuit of success and are motivated about your goals. The gas is the driving force in the car, just like your passion gets you up in the morning and pursuing your dreams.

You start to drive and you keep on driving, just like how you should keep on persisting towards your goals. Driving the car, you see that you have ended up at the Louisiana state line. You have made a mistake and are not where you want to be. Too often in real life when this happens you might say, "I give up. I am in the wrong place. *I have failed.*"

What you should say in these cases is, "Why did I go the wrong way? How did I get here? Where did I take the wrong turn? Where do I need to make a change?" You need to ask those questions and learn from your mistakes.

"When you ended up in Louisiana, have you failed?"

The answer is no, you have not failed. You just went the wrong way. Get back in the car, get directions, and drive. Continue to strive for your goal. So you get back in your car and drive some more. After awhile, you discover that you are in Florida instead of Maine. Have you failed? Not really. Maybe you have learned that you are a very poor map-reader and have learned to ask directions more frequently.

If you learn and take everything along the way as input, there is no such thing as failure. Just keep on going because you believe you can get there, that you can get to Maine. If you keep striving for your goals with this mind set, you will enjoy the journey in getting there … and you will get there in the end. Life brings turns and curves and problems, but it is how we overcome them and act upon them that make us successful.

This may be a funny example, but it is so real in life. This shows how we sometimes react to obstacles in life. Just be smart by making a decision from which you will learn with each and every experience in life, and I promise you it will make a difference. You will like the outcomes of your attitude and most often the end result.

Life is challenging. It brings struggles you will have to face, overcome, and learn from in order to be successful in life. Will you learn from each and every experience? I hope your answer is "Yes".

No matter what, keep on going ...

"Will *you* pay the price for success?"

"Are *you* willing to do what you have to do, when you don't want to do it?"

"Do you believe *you* can do it?"

It is vital to develop actions that are consistent and ongoing. Just as you need to learn from each and every experience, you need to keep on going during hard times. You need to persevere every day towards your dreams and goals. Just being persistent will help you accomplish many of your goals. When you keep on persisting, four outcomes occur:

1) You create more success.
2) You keep yourself accountable.
3) You develop momentum.
4) You gain the perspective of expecting the best.

Keep Focused ... And Revisit Your Plan Daily

What do I mean when I say that you create more success when you keep on going and persisting?

You create more potential for success when you are focused because you are able to see new ideas and possibilities. You are able to take advantage of these new ideas and possibilities. Sometimes things just fall right into place or right into your lap.

Recently this happened for me. I was focused on my Soaring Eagles program that helps young adults live life on purpose, with purpose.

I was focused on creating an awesome business for young adults, but my strategy at that time in getting new members was not working very well. I was marketing this Soaring Eagles program all over the country. One day I caught on to a new idea as I was speaking to the principal of a school. Because of our discussion, I was able to come speak to his students. Many of his students joined Soaring Eagles, and I was able to influence more students, getting closer to my goal of influencing 1,500 young adults by 2005. I am not there yet, but with this avenue I will accomplish it more quickly.

I could have gotten discouraged about the program and I could have decided not to pursue getting new members. If I had done that, I would not have spoken with the principal and I would not have gotten the new members I did. I got them simply because I had opened myself up for new possibilities.

When you are motivated and excited about life, many other opportunities pop up. That is what I mean when I say you create more success when you keep on persisting. If you try it, I promise you will like the results.

Being persistent means you are being disciplined in accomplishing your goal, in accomplishing the task you have set out to do. Discipline is the connection from one side of the bridge to the other side, just like having a goal and accomplishing it.

> "Envy is the mud that those who fail throw at the those who succeed."
> — Anonymous

Many people are envious of others who have accomplished things in their lives because they personally have not. But being persistent, being focused on your goal and consistently striving to reach it is why you will succeed when others do not.

My definition of persistence is this: Persistence is the personal focus that only sees opportunities or possibilities; it does not see obstacles. So decide right now to be persistent in pursuing your goal and not be envious of others.

How does persistence keep you accountable?

When you keep on going by holding yourself accountable in accomplishing what you have set out to do, it develops discipline. If you strive every day for your goals, it shows you are holding yourself accountable for your future, not depending on anyone else to do it for you. When you hold yourself accountable, you are in control of your life.

My father, Clifford, taught me this. When he would start a job, he held himself accountable for accomplishing his task and never stopped until he was done. You never had to ask my dad twice to get the work done. As my father would work around our house, he wouldn't stop until it was finished. Being accountable keeps and builds your work ethic.

Keep Focused ... And Revisit Your Plan Daily

My father taught me that I needed to take control of my life because nobody else would. My destiny depended on my striving for my wants in life. You will make yourself successful if you keep yourself accountable.

As you keep on going you also develop and establish momentum ...

Many people seeking a goal begin to establish momentum, only to rest and watch TV when it's the best time to forge ahead. The best time to go harder is when you have momentum because at that time you have more push.

When momentum is on your side, it is so much easier to succeed. The best friend of an achiever or a goal-oriented person is momentum. In leading the Soaring Eagles Division, I have tried to create momentum in acquiring new members because I know how important it is. I have been putting on seminars and marketing differently to create momentum. Because of this momentum, it is easier to acquire new members.

Whatever you do in life, create momentum.

Expecting the best

As you persist on your path, holding yourself accountable, creating more success and momentum, make sure to expect the best. I know it is often hard to expect good things because when you do, you feel you are being greedy. What I mean is to believe and think that if you keep on doing something in a positive direction, something good will come out of it.

Expect the best to rise up. Have the mind set and knowledge to understand that you will receive what you expect.

Reviewing your goals on a regular basis is extremely helpful in accomplishing what you want. It helps keep your mind focused on the target, and it aligns your thinking. So, develop the habit of checking out your goals on a regular basis.

And remember that you are never pursuing your goal alone; there are other influences that help you along the way, influences such as momentum, ambition, focus, drive, happiness, motivation, and others.

Chapter 4

"Choose someone fun ...

... to help you along your journey."

In this chapter you will learn:
- How to keep yourself accountable for your own success by letting others help you;
- How to make your goals clearer and more real;
- Why you should choose a coach or a mentor.

Do you have someone to help you? Do you have someone to encourage you? Do you have a helper?

If you don't, I recommend that you choose someone to help you along your life journey. It makes reaching your goals—and ultimately enjoying life more fully—a lot easier. A mentor or a coach is an amazing boost to living life more successfully. Why is this so?

I have learned from hundreds of people that you can do more and achieve more with a team than by yourself. You can move the biggest obstacles or climb Mt. Everest with a team, but these same tasks can be impossible by yourself. Great things that will make a huge difference in people's lives for years to come are going to be done by teams of people working together and not by individuals. Even someone as dedicated to personal responsibility and individual action as Mother Theresa worked willingly as part of a group to make the changes in the world she did.

That is why a coach or mentor is such an important part of your success plan. (While coaches and mentors are not quite the same, I use the terms interchangeably in my discussion here).

Your mentor could be someone who is directly involved with your actual dream. Or it could be a person who is on the outside giving you advice from their perspective. Having a mentor is definitely a win/win situation for you both. The mentor gets to help you achieve something that is important in your life, giving him or her a feeling of accomplishment. And you get personal development, a feeling of belonging, and a feeling of mutual respect.

You want to have coaches who are honest with their feedback. Sometimes they have to give you feedback that doesn't sound good, and sometimes it hurts, but you need that advice and you should be happy that they give it to you. We all know we are not perfect. We need to be open and learn from what others see and make necessary changes. You should actively pursue that advice because we all walk around in life with blind spots. Your coach will help you see those blind spots so that you develop greater and faster success.

I have had many mentors in my life, but let me share with you what I have received from a few of them.

One of my mentors is Denny Magnuson who lives in San Diego, California.

Mr. Magnuson is a very successful businessman. He guided me and shaped me in becoming a better person. Sometimes he would give me input, and sometimes it would hurt, but I needed to hear it. He always told me the truth, and I needed to change what he called my attention to.

My father, Clifford, is another great mentor in life. When I was growing up I called him MacGyver (and I call him that today) because he always seems to know how to do everything. He mentored me both in work (such as construction and electrical) and in work ethics (such as being persistent, never giving up, focusing on the task, helping others, and being kind). He also mentored me in sports and helped me develop my football skills. He would go out with me almost every day and throw the football to me because he knew "practice makes permanent," that what is practiced and worked on becomes second nature. He taught me techniques in catching the ball better. One drill he had me do was to catch the tennis ball that he would throw high, very high, up in the air, up as high as he could. This forced me to concentrate and focus, and once I learned those skills, I could catch it.

My brother Ryan is another one of my important mentors, again primarily in sports. I looked forward to him giving me guidance in sports and loved when he did. He played football at Cal Poly, San Luis Obispo and was all conference his first year as a kick-off returner. He is only 5'5", but he has a big heart and a lot of talent.

Ryan would give me guidance about different moves or techniques to get away from defenders. Most important, he helped me with the mental side of football. Some of his advice felt good, particularly when he was complimenting me when I did things well. Some of his input didn't feel that good. I didn't like hearing that I wasn't doing things correctly, but I needed to hear it even if I didn't like it. Ryan brought the best out of me in sports.

When by brother was a senior in high school and I was a sophomore, he played on varsity team while I played on the sophomore team. My games were always before his, so after every one of my games I would run over and give him support for all the support he had given me. His mentoring was coming back to him. It was a win/win interaction.

If you have a mentor and he or she has made a positive difference in your life—like my brother and many others have in mine—you will understand what its like to have one and why having a coach is so powerful, life changing, and beneficial.

Choose Someone Fun ... To Help You Along on Your Journey

Another mentor I currently have is John C. Maxwell, a great speaker and author. John doesn't even know that he has influenced me as much as he has and how much he will in the future. I only spoke to him once, but I constantly listen to his tapes and read his books. This is another way someone can mentor you.

Sometimes you might have a team of mentors. I have a team of mentors right now. Bill and Joann Truby are two people mentoring me about business techniques, ideas, and strategies in the Soaring Eagles Division.

Things to remember when finding a mentor and being mentored:

1) You need to initiate the contact with the mentor;
2) Keep open to input, because everything doesn't always sound good;
3) Find someone you can trust who will give you honest feedback and who knows and supports what you want to be;
4) Maintain the attitude of wanting to grow and learn when you meet with your coach;
5) And, make sure you enjoy your time together.

Having a mentor helps you in your journey in these ways:

1) **Makes your goals clearer.** When you tell somebody else that you will accomplish something, it makes you clarify your goals for yourself. If you are able to speak clearly about your goals and dreams, it makes them clearer in your own mind. When your mind is clear, it is easier to be focused on attaining your goals.

2) **Makes your goals easier.** When you talk about your goals, it makes attaining them seem easier. If you were only to think about climbing Mt. Everest, it seems like a huge endeavor. But if you say to someone else, "I will climb Mt. Everest," it seems easier. It actually is no easier, but having said it, it seems to be. You try it. Think about something that is quite big. Then say it out loud; it doesn't seem quite so big anymore.

3) **Keeps you accountable.** When you tell someone that you are going to do something, there is another driving force that helps you to accomplish your dreams. Another person will say, "Have you done that?" It is a great feeling when you say "yes." And if you say, "no," it will drive you even more, beyond your personal drive.

Do you have a mentor in mind?

If you do, go ask kindly for guidance. If you need a mentor in life, and you don't have one and can't think of one, I could fulfill that need with the Soaring Eagles. I have included a contact number at the end of the book.

Chapter 5

"Don't just walk ...

... leap to success."

In this chapter you will learn:
- How to enjoy the work and the process;
- How to understand and develop a balanced life;
- How to live a balanced life and that balance is a matter of choice.

Do you feel overwhelmed with work and with what you need to do? Or do you have adventure or action in your life? Are you living a life of happiness?

My brother, Ryan, attends Palmer College, in Santa Clara while he lives in San Jose. Palmer College is a chiropractic school, and one of the best. He is an example of someone who lives life to the fullest.

Listen to this ...

Ryan is on a 3-year program to get his degree and the knowledge to be able to have his own chiropractic practice. He is currently taking 31 units a semester, which he will be doing for each of the semesters during these three years. This means he is in classes Monday through Friday from 7 A.M. to 4 P.M.

His classes are really difficult. It is even difficult to say the titles or pronounce the words on the cover of his books. The most units that I have taken, at U.C. Davis, were 18 units and I felt slammed and overwhelmed.

This seems like too much work for many people. How can he enjoy that process? When I talk to Ryan, I can tell he is overloaded at times, but I know that he is enjoying the process. He is enjoying the process of becoming a chiropractor because that is his passion. But more importantly, he is living a balanced life. That is the key. Let me share with you what I mean when I say he is living a balanced life.

Living a balanced life

There are various lists from different disciplines, teachings or experts. There are seven areas of life that need to be fulfilled in order for you to live life happily, less stressed, and more positively. Ryan makes sure he lives his life fully in all seven areas of life. And it is important that you do so also.

The seven areas of life as taught by the Truby Achievement Center are:

- Mental
- Physical
- Recreational
- Emotional
- Professional
- Spiritual
- Relational

Ryan understands the dynamics of living a balanced life and the effect doing so can have on our lives if we do live them equally. In the Bible, John 10, says, " ... I have come that they may have life, and have it to the full." I believe God is saying that we all need to live life fully, that we should live a balanced life, and that we should live life to the fullest.

When Ryan has breaks from school, he makes sure he has some fun like surfing. He is always under pressure taking exams, and he knows if he is happier he will do better. He is on a break right now in Cabo San Lucas surfing, relaxing, and recreating. He is making sure that he is having fun. He has two weeks off and is spending one week in Cabo and one week at home.

For the last week he is determined to fulfill the other areas. In regards to his physical part, he already works out every day. He will fulfill the relational aspect by spending time with his family and his girlfriend. His emotional area will be fulfilled with those friends and family members. He sees to being fulfilled in his spiritual aspect every day. His professional aspect is fulfilled by studying business marketing techniques and systems for chiropractic practices.

If one of these seven areas is not being fulfilled, it will affect the other areas of your life. When you are out of balance in any one of them, your entire life will seem out of whack also, even if they are not. This is a common cause of "burn out."

Definitions of the 7 areas

Here are definitions provided by the Truby Achievement Center, so you can make sure you are living life fulfilled in all areas.

- The *mental area* is the area of your life where you are mentally challenged or participate in activities that make you think.
- The *physical area* has to do with any aspect of your physiology – from nutrition to exercise.
- The *spiritual area* is the spiritual force, connection and support of a higher power.
- The *recreational area* is where you have fun or recreate yourself.
- The *relational area* is where you interact with other humans in positive ways.
- The *professional area* is where you apply yourself in work.
- And lastly, the *emotional area* encompasses personal feelings you need to be in touch with others and yourself.

So, are you living your life fulfilled in all these areas?

What do I mean exactly by being fulfilled?

Think of life as being a circle or a wheel on a wagon. The diagram on the next page represents what I mean.

If all the slices of this diagram are the same shape and size, they fit together to make a perfect circle. If they were not the same size, then the circle would not be round. Just like if a wheel had spokes that were different lengths, the wheel wouldn't roll smoothly and would break. It would go around and hit where the circle is not perfect, creating a bumpy ride.

Each area of your life needs to be equal and balanced. You could

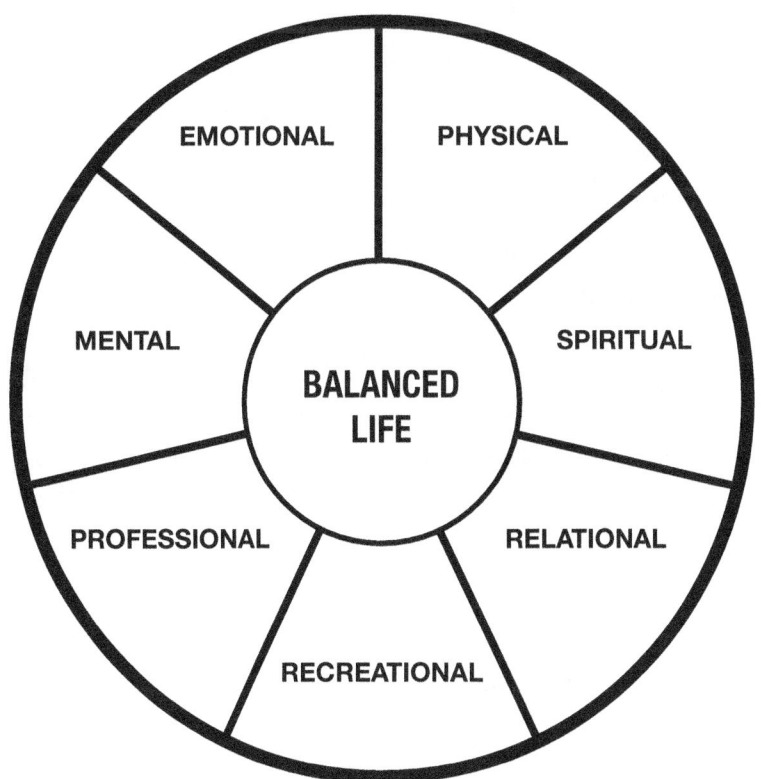

measure it on a scale from 1 to 10, with 1 being the lowest (not fulfilled) and 10 the highest (completely fulfilled). The diagram above is an example of living life fully, living life at a 10 level for each area.

Where do you see yourself in these areas? You should assess your life right now and decide how balanced a life you are living. There are no real criteria for the numbers. They come from inside you. You will know if an area is a 3 or a 5 or a 10. You will be able to feel it.

For example, let's say you are living life in each area below with the following ratings:

Recreational	=	10
Emotional	=	9
Professional	=	10
Spiritual	=	9
Mental	=	10
Physical	=	2
Relational	=	10

Your wheel would roll pretty smoothly until it hit the Physical area, which is only a 2. You are not living life fulfilled in that area. For you to be living fulfilled, it should be a 10.

With this 2, the wheel would roll, then plop, roll then plop again, and on and on. If you needed to push the wagon, it would be very hard for you. So we need to have all areas of life equally fulfilled to be happy.

What are your personal numbers in each area of your life?

If some area is low, how do you raise it?

If the physical aspect is low in your life, all you need to do is increase it by making time for it. If you say you are too busy to fit it in, try to fit it in when you are doing something else. For instance, when you are thinking or strategizing about business, you can walk on the treadmill or walk around the block for exercise.

Whatever area you are lacking in, it is necessary to put it somewhere in your busy schedule. If you need to balance the physical aspect of your life, you can get a membership in a gym or a personal trainer. This helps particularly if your problem is motivation and not time. But the important thing is to make the choice to fulfill this area of your life in some way so that you can bring your entire life back into balance. It is amazing, too, how pulling the low parts of your life back into balance affects all parts of your life and makes everything seem to be balanced and roll smoothly.

Things to remember to live a balanced life:
1) Choose to want to live a balanced life: First you need to make the decision;
2) Choose how you will implement the area where you are lacking;
3) Then, take action;
4) Approach all of the above points with a positive attitude.

Do you want to live a balanced life?

If you do, just make the choice to do so. And then develop actions that will fulfill the areas that are out of whack. With just a few adjustments in your life, you will receive the benefit of feeling fulfilled if you had been living a life that is unbalanced.

108

Chapter 6

"Overcoming your obstacles ...
... You can make it easy."

In this chapter you will learn:
- What your obstacles are;
- How to develop and plan a flow chart for success;
- What can hold you back;
- How to handle your stress.

Do you ever have anything that gets in your way of accomplishing something? Of course you do. Does it happen often? Do you want to change that? Do you want to overcome your obstacles?

Well, you can with a simple and effective system I will share with you. You will be able to use a tool that has worked for me and many others. It's as simple as this: You increase your chances of overcoming your obstacles with proper preparation and planning.

<u>Success comes in how you react to life's obstacles</u>. A life truth is that you won't overcome every obstacle, but with your attitude towards them, you can overcome their ability to stop you in your quest for your dreams. If you use this approach, you will overcome your obstacles with a higher percentage than you've had in the past.

Some obstacles are more formidable than others. But that does not mean they cannot be overcome.

The only difference between a roadblock (obstacle) and a stepping stone (goal) is the way you think about them and whether you allow them to stop you or if you learn from them. Your attitude and perspective are the keys.

So would you like to overcome your obstacles with a higher percentage than you've had in the past?

If you do, the simple tool I'm about to show will let you focus on just how to change obstacles into steppingstones.

How to overcome your obstacles ...

I was speaking recently to my awesome grandpa Jack Steen about how I was writing and publishing a book on setting goals. I shared with him that I only had two more chapters left in finishing the book and that I was working on the chapter about overcoming obstacles or roadblocks in life.

My grandpa is such a character and is so funny. He responded by asking me if I wanted to know how to get rid of my obstacles.

I said, "Yes, tell me".

He said, "You first get rid of your wife, then your kids, then your girlfriend, then your second girlfriend, and then your third girlfriend."

And then with a big smile on his face, he said, "There go all your obstacles. You won't have them anymore; they're all gone."

We laughed for at least 15 minutes.

I don't suggest you do what my grandpa recommended. Let me show you a better way to overcome your obstacles. The tool is basically about planning and developing what you will do when you have an obstacle in the way of a specific outcome. After using it, obstacles you have had in the past will be easier to overcome.

Anything's Possible! Chapter 6

Here is the tool ...

First, you make a flow chart, like this:

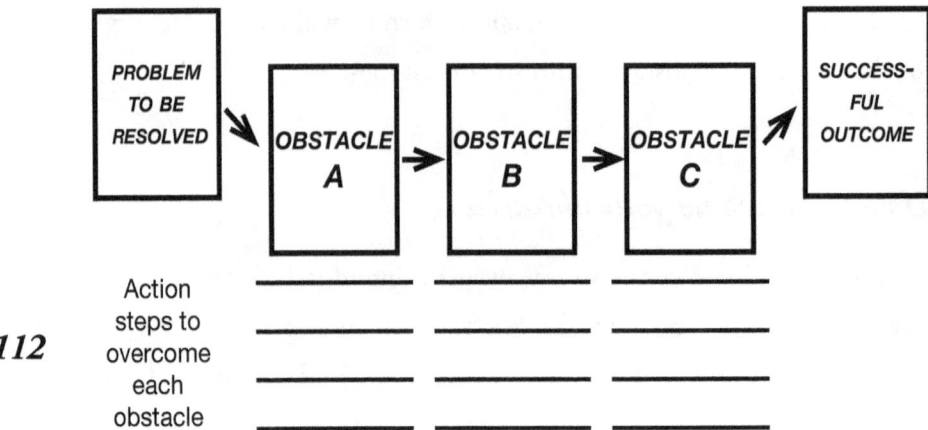

This is the layout you use. Your problem starts on the left and the successful outcome is on the right. Your obstacles to overcoming the problem are in boxes A, B, C.

The action steps under A, B, and C are things that you do to overcome each obstacle A, B or C.

Now, here is a specific example for you ...

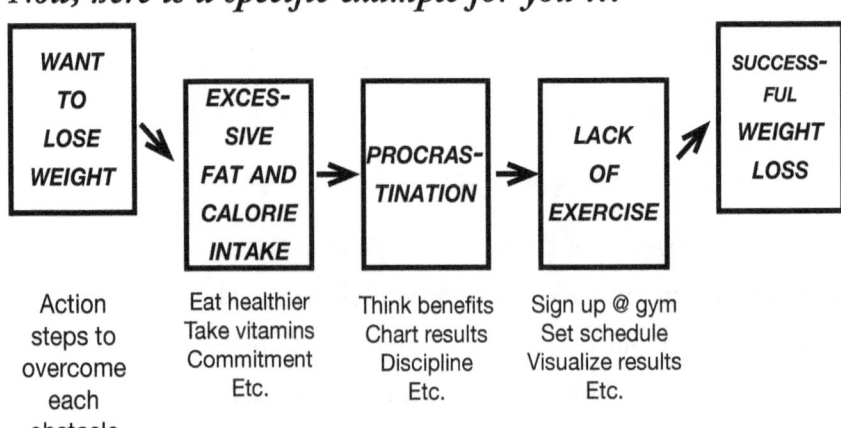

Box A (excessive fat and calorie intake): The action steps you take to overcome eating too much are to make the decision to eat healthier, take vitamins, and make a commitment.

Box B: (procrastination): The action steps you take to overcome are to think benefits, chart results, and develop discipline.

Box C: (lack of resources): The action steps to take in overcoming this problem are to sign up at a gym, think about the value you will receive, use it four times/week, and find the importance of why you are doing this by visualizing results.

These action steps overcome the three obstacles that you might have in losing weight.

Now you try it

We have a blank flow chart for you to use on the next page. Fill in the boxes and lines just like above, but with your particular obstacles. Then fill in the action steps you will take to overcome A, B, and C.

What are some things that can hold you back?

There's a statement in the bible that reads: "Consider it pure joy when you face trials of many kinds, knowing that the testing of your faith develops perseverance, that perseverance once achieved brings you to maturity, complete and not lacking in anything" (James 1:2-4). This quotation has many important points, but I think the most important is when trial comes, we actually build from that trial in life something better than we were.

I have encountered obstacles in my own life of course. Maybe you have encountered similar ones, so you might be able to learn from my

Anything's Possible! Chapter 6

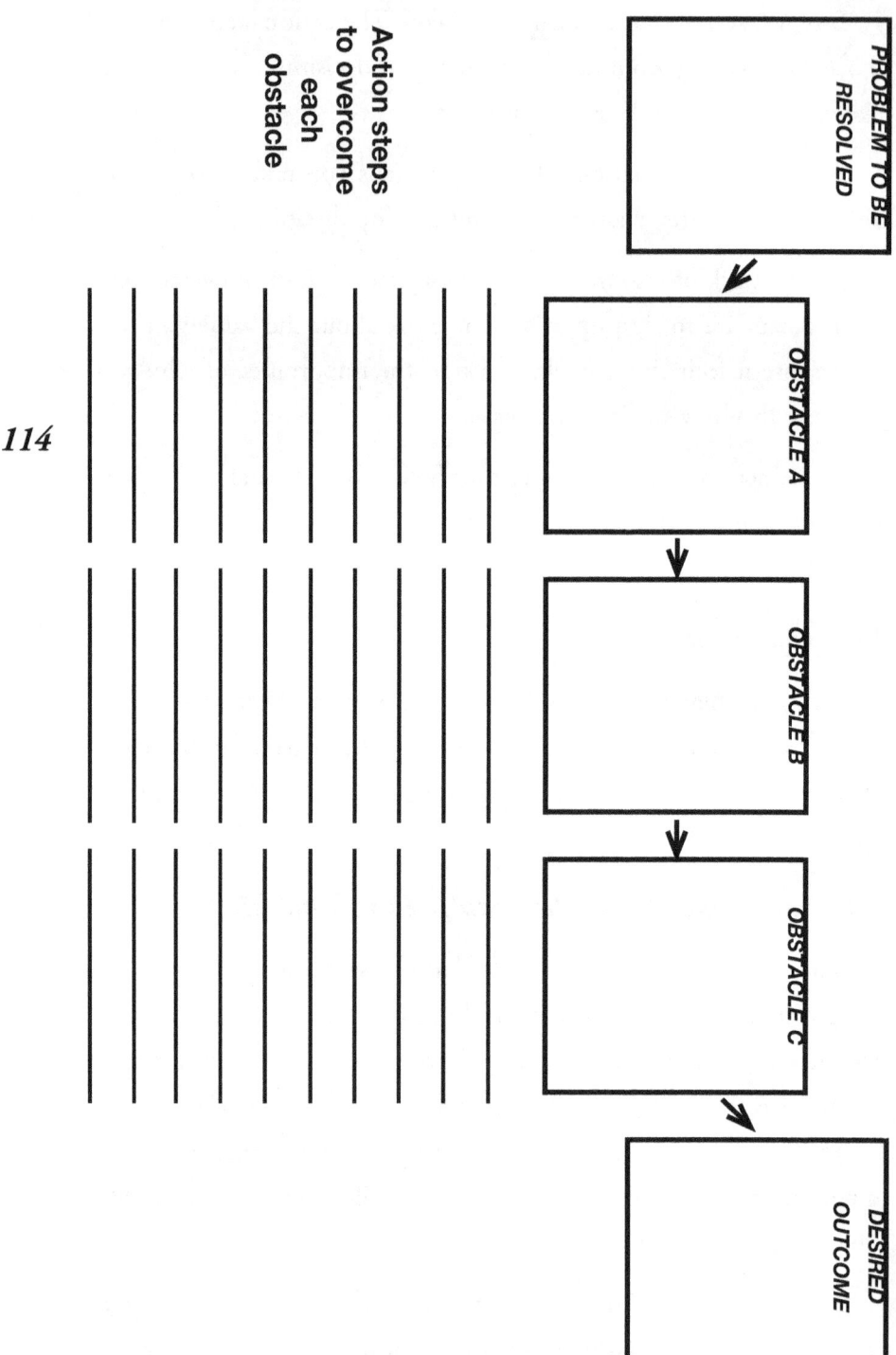

experience. Here are a few of the things that could have held me—or anybody—back:

- Personal belief
- Learned helplessness
- Lack of discipline
- Lack of focus
- Fear of failure
- Setting goals too high
- Letting other people knock you down
- Lack of perseverance and persistence
- Not fulfilling the 7 areas of life equally

1) *Personal Belief*

Do you ever say, "Can I do this? Should I even try?" If you say these things consistently, you need to find the belief in yourself that you are a valuable person (remember the self-esteem issues?), that you are great, and that you can achieve what you want.

I shared with you in the first chapter how important it is to believe in yourself. If you don't believe you can accomplish something, then you won't. I guarantee it. And I can guarantee that if you *do* believe in yourself, you *will* accomplish what you set out to do.

Another area where personal belief is important is how you see yourself and your perspective about life.

Your perspective comes down to your belief. What you see is what you think you can do. The example from my life happened when I finished my football days at high school in Napa, California. My brother attended Cal Poly, and I wanted to go to the same school and play football with him. That was one of my dreams and it happened.

I was at the Cal Poly training camp, double days, on the football team. Long story short is that my perspective from what I had played in high school was completely different after only two weeks of college. The difference in the playing level and experience was amazing.

I went back to Napa after two weeks and wished I had had the same perspective while playing high school ball that I learned in college. I would have done so much better.

"Curtis, are you saying that you could have done better just being with college players in only two weeks time?"

Yes, I could have. Not because I was stronger, or faster, or better. It was entirely that I had a bigger and better perspective. My standards went up a notch. In high school I ran timidly compared to how I ran in college. And all that really had changed was my perspective.

Your perspective and belief should help you attain your goals. Do not let them hinder you as they did me in high school football. Your perspective is a powerful tool you can use for your benefit. We both know that two people can be in the same exact place, and come out of that place with totally different thoughts and opinions of what they saw.

Here is a true story about a high school English class that illustrates the point perfectly. The teacher was about to give a test to 22 students. The students were nervous because she said that this test was the hardest one she was ever going to give that year. She said that previous year, only four students out of 40 had passed. Then she said, "If there are students who don't want to take this exam and want to leave now, I will give a B to those students who leave."

Most students said, "Yes, I am out of here. I'll take a B. There's nothing wrong with a B."

All but 7 students left. These students were ready for the challenge.

What would you have done? Would you have stayed or would you have left?

They wanted to take that test because they had prepared and they believed in themselves. Then the teacher said this, "Are you seven students ready for the test?"

Students together said, "Yes, we are."

Teacher said, "Great, go home. You seven have received an A on this test because each of you believed in yourself."

Develop that kind of belief, and you will be ready for—and excited about—any challenge you face.

2) "Learned Helplessness"

"Learned Helplessness" means that you have learned to be helpless in life. If you learned in the past from parents, teachers, peers or other important people in your life that you couldn't do something or accomplish goals, and now you think that you can't do it in the present or in the future—that's learned helplessness.

Don't let this happen to you. No matter what you have done, the past has no influence on what you can do in the future. If you got a bad grade on a test, this test has no influence on what you can do on the next test. Certainly, you can learn from it, but it won't have an overriding influence on succeeding with the next one unless you let it.

Learned helplessness is like the way flies trapped in a jar behave. Imagine a large group of flies in a sealed gallon jar. When the flies first try to escape, they keep on bumping against the cap. Sooner or later, they will not fly up to the cap anymore. Even when the cap is eventually removed, they do not fly upward; they have learned that they can't get out. They have learned to be helpless.

> "This is one thing I do, forgetting those things that are behind, and reaching forth unto those things that are before."
> — Philippians 3:13

When I was young, I learned to be helpless in school. Remember my story about the special teacher I attended while other students were in the regular class.

I was not effective doing anything in school because of my difficulties in one subject. Because of that, I learned that I couldn't do anything academic. My English got worse because I learned that I shouldn't even try after the incident that embarrassed me when I left class scared and made fun off. I was like a hermit crab that wouldn't come out of its shell.

I was too scared to try anything academic because I had learned how to be helpless. Instead of learning helplessness, we need—you need—to learn how to let go of things that you couldn't accomplish in the past and look instead to the future as if you are starting new.

Victor Frankel was a survivor of the Nazi concentration camps. Mr. Frankel has related how the Nazis would beat the prisoners, yell at them, and would tell them that they would die. Abusing them psychologically with words and physically with beatings, the Nazis tried to wear down the prisoners.

Mr. Frankel said when prisoners would lose hope and didn't want to get out of bed was the day they would die. He said that he never lost hope and he believed that he would get out. Mr. Frankel never learned how to be helpless. When you lose hope for the future, you have learned to be helpless.

There is a great book, called the *Adversity Quotient* by Paul Stoltz. Mr. Stoltz writes about what adversity is and how to overcome it. He also talks extensively about "Learned Helplessness." I highly recommend reading it. It is life changing, and he is the expert.

3) Lack of Discipline

In hard times, do you stop? Do you stop when you really want to keep on going? Or do you persist on your path toward your goal?

Words like discipline, sacrifice, patience, and perseverance are easy words to say but hard words to live by. They are hard because they mean hard work and keeping on when times are tough.

Whatever is not accomplished today, comes on us tomorrow. When we are not disciplined in what we have to do or what we want, the difficulty we face doesn't just go away, it comes the next day. It never leaves us. Being disciplined in your habits, disciplined in your emotions, disciplined in your thoughts are the real keys to being successful. I know that persistence and discipline will take you just as far as knowledge or talents.

When I played football at U.C. Davis, we had "double days" in the beginning of the year. Double days meant we had two practices per day, one in the morning and one in the afternoon, and we would have to wake up early for the first practice each day at 6 o'clock in the morning. Double days were very intense and very tiring. I was so sore that I would have to sit in a bathtub full of ice. That is how sore everybody was.

Some people would get there late, and because of their lack of discipline, the whole team would have to run a lot. One person's lack of discipline would affect many others not just himself. One individual's lack of discipline could affect the whole team, and that got people going around to the dorms to make sure and wake all the team up so they would get there on time.

> "When people are put into positions slightly above what they would expect, they are apt to excel."
> — Richard Branson

Did you see the great movie, *Remember the Titans?* If so, you remember the fight between the stars on the team when they first went to camp. Because of their lack of discipline—their not making the right choices to respect each other—the head coach took them on a run in the middle of the night.

I personally never had to do that, but their lack of discipline resulted in serious consequences. Just like when I had to run extra when somebody lacked the discipline to get to practice on time.

There are three areas in which you need to establish discipline.

The first area is to have disciplined thoughts. Positive thinking about what you want is the key to attaining your dreams.

The second area is to have disciplined habits, to keep on going no matter what hits you in the face.

The last area is to have disciplined emotions. When you can control your emotions, they will not control you.

So if you want to succeed in reaching your dreams, choose to be disciplined in all of these areas.

Here are some inspiring thoughts from John C. Maxwell about discipline:

"Honesty and frankness make you vulnerable.
    Be honest and frank anyway.
If you are successful, you will win false friends and true enemies.
    Succeed anyway.
What we spend years building may be destroyed overnight.
    Build anyway.
People really need help but may attack you if you help them.
    Help them anyway.
Give the world the best you've got and you'll get kicked in the teeth.
    Give the world the best you've got anyway."

Now you can see how he can be a great mentor.

4) Lack of focus

Just as focus is a strength in accomplishing your wants, the lack of focus is a weakness that can keep you from accomplishing *anything*. Being focused will get you to your target just as fast and as surely as talent and ability. Faster, even. Keeping focused on the target will get you where you want to go.

Why did I make the point that you should review your goals three times daily? It is for this reason: Reviewing your goals frequently encourages focus. By reviewing your goals on a regular basis, you will not lack focus because you are constantly thinking and looking over your goals and dreams.

In my life, I have noticed a huge difference when I reviewed my goals instead of when I didn't review my goals. Well, what happened?

This is what happened when I **didn't** review my goals. And this can ... and will ... happen to you:

- I would start to do things that were off-task or counter to my needs.
- I would procrastinate more.
- I would focus only on playing and not working.
- If someone asked me, "What are your goals?" I couldn't even answer.
- I was not happy and did not looking forward to the future.
- I didn't accomplish anything of significance.

On the other hand, this is what happens when I **do** review my goals on a regular basis:

- I am on task and more productive.
- I don't procrastinate.
- I know where I am going. I am focused.
- I am excited and pumped up about the future.
- I am happier.
- I am more effective ... and more successful.

5) *Fear of failure*

There is no such thing as failure ... if, and only if, you take everything along the way as input. You can make mistakes, but if you learn from each and every experience in life, you will be constantly growing. Life is an endless road until you leave it; you really cannot fail if you keep persisting along that road.

Remember when I said how I was scared to give speeches in front of people and that now I have decreased my fear? I was able to do so because I want my dream more than I want to listen to my fears. Your fear will cost you more in all aspects of life compared to striving for your dream.

Success has a high price, but failure, at least what most people call "failure," will cost you more. Failure will cost you the embarrassment of not accomplishing something, while success costs you the work and persistence in getting there. Which would you rather choose?

One of my mentors, John C. Maxwell, teaches people that they need to *fail forward*—or to learn from your experience in failing. He wrote a book on this, which I highly recommend.

If you start to fail or have failed, it is best to fail forward. It is not if you will fail because you will. We all have difficulties. It is how you fail that makes the difference. Are you failing forward, learning from your mistakes? Or are you failing backwards and not getting up? That is true failure.

What I got out of John Maxwell's book is that you need to learn from your experiences, looking at your mistakes as a learning experience. If you fail backwards, you are giving up and not learning from your failures.

But you and I know there is no such thing as failure if you take everything along the way as input.

Remember the analogy of driving from California to Maine?

There really is no way you can fail—even if you end up in the wrong place—if you learn why you went the wrong way. Just take everything in as input. I truly believe that there is no such thing as failure if you keep on going, learning, and coming back again.

6) Setting goals too high

What do I mean by setting goals too high?

If you set your goals too high or completely out of your reach, they will be unattainable and thus frustrate you. If you set goals that are too low, they will not stretch you enough. Remember in Chapter 2, point #5 on how to Set Goals Effectively is to set them realistically, but also make them a stretch.

My personal example was how I wanted to buy a house. I thought I could get it earlier, but the prices of houses are unbelievable. I was stretching myself too much at that point in time. Later, I know it will be easier.

Life example: I played college football and did pretty well, but right now it is unattainable to say I could play on the NFL. Furthermore, it will become even more unattainable as I get older. If I set a goal to play on the NFL, that would be an example of my setting a goal that is too high. It is very hard to set a goal that is too small, one that won't achieve your dream and your goal because it is the small steps that get you to your overall dreams.

7) Letting other people knock you down

When you are striving for your goals, you might come across someone telling you that you can't do it, or that you shouldn't do it, or that you can't make it. And why is this so? Why will people try to hold you back?

People become weird when you are striving for something while they aren't. There really are only a few people who are working towards an awesome future like you are. When you are going for the gold, some people will try to say you are not doing what you should be doing, or that you won't make it, or you can't do it.

These people are jealous that you might make it to the top. When you attain or are meaningfully trying to reach your goal, some people will try—though maybe not consciously—to hold you back. Some people will tell you that you shouldn't try to accomplish something out of the love they feel for you. Family members might say you shouldn't work to actualize your dream, even if you want it, not out of disrespect but out of love. For example, family and friends will say they are trying to protect you from failure. They are scared that you will fail because success is so hard to achieve. But you have learned that there is no such thing as real failure if you fail forward. They may want to protect you from failure or challenges, but they are really preventing you from succeeding. A reality of success is this: Most people are not successful if they haven't experienced and overcome challenges in life.

Life is all about challenges and struggles you have to overcome. And without those challenges, you will not be truly successful. So in this perspective, family and friends who try to protect you from failure are hurting you more than when you are allowed to strive and potentially mess up. Being hurt temporarily by obstacles that lay in the middle of the road will be worth it if you get up again and keep going because if you stop because of the obstacles, you certainly will never succeed.

8) *Lack of perseverance and persistence*

You first have to go through the dirt in order to get to the gold. Being persistent in your actions will bring more success than you can imagine.

My father Clifford was a good example of perseverance. When he would have a goal or a task, he would work diligently on it until it was completed. It was indeed an amazing sight to watch my father work around the house. He would keep on going on a project for days until he finished it to his high standards.

I remember this one project I had in elementary school. I was supposed to build a small house that would be put on a board that would be graded by the teacher. The board had to be 2 feet by 2 feet. I asked my father for help, and he said he would.

This is no joke; he worked on that house for 10 days straight from 6 P.M. when he got back from work until one or even later in the early morning. He did my work, which was bad, but his perseverance was awesome to see and he taught me how to be persistent.

This house was not normal. It was so elegant and precise. He had used small pieces of paper as shingles on the roof. It looked exactly like a house. It had a little door that opened with a mat in front of the door that said, "Welcome." It had a deck that was miniature in size, a chimney that came from in the house through the roof.

Well, you get the point. There was so much to it you can probably guess what grade I received on it. Put it this way: Nobody had a better house than I did.

He showed me how persistence pays off in the long run.

9) *Not living balanced in all the areas of life …*

Remember how you need to live fulfilled in all the seven areas of life to be balanced, effective and happy. If you do not do this, you will end up hindering yourself in accomplishing anything. My mother would stress this as I was growing up. She would say, "Take a break from your work and eat," or "Go have fun and play."

Without happiness and enjoyment you will not even want to go through what you need to be successful.

The seven areas again are these:

- Emotional
- Physical
- Mental
- Spiritual
- Professional
- Relational
- Recreational

You need to fulfill these areas of your life equally. Go back to Chapter 5 to find out how to fulfill all these areas of life that need to be fulfilled.

Here is a personal example. My parents went through a divorce. I am a family man, and I love spending time with family. When I went to Cal Poly, I drove home almost every week for the year that I went there, four and a half hours one way to be with my family. I did it not because I was homesick but just because I wanted to be with my family.

When I found out my parents were getting a divorce, it devastated me. My life was really messed up for about a year because of this. Everything else seemed out of whack because my relational area of life was out of whack.

It wasn't just one area of my life that was messed up. The problems in one area affected all of my life.

Things that were going on with me in that year:

I was not happy.

I lost weight and muscle because I did not feel like working out.

I didn't play my last year of football at Davis.

It was hard for me to trust people.

My spiritual life went on the fritz.

I had no goals in life.

I was angry at the world.

So, quite simply, I was a mess. One area of my life rated a zero, and it influenced me in all the other areas. As soon as I understood that all of these problems were happening because one area was not right, I was able to take back control by fulfilling my relational area. Everything changed 180 degrees. I was happy; I was gaining muscle; I was able to trust, and so on.

Make sure you live life fully in all the seven areas of life.

How to overcome your stress

I know you've been stressed out at least once in your life. And if you're "normal," it's been a lot more than that. Does stress overwhelm you, or can you handle it effectively?

Remember, circumstances do not make us what we are, they reveal what we are. So, how you handle your stress is important in your life. Your attitude is the key, not the circumstance itself.

All our lives seem like this. I have a meeting at the office at 8 A.M.; at 8:15 I have an appointment until 9 A.M. Then I have a hair appointment at 9:15, need to go to the bank at 10, meet Joe at 10:30, I need to go buy this and then meet that person, and on and on.

Does this sound like your life? It probably does, because people's lives are busy.

That is a very important reason to plan what you want so you can be more effective, more efficient, and quicker in getting things accomplished. This will happen if you plan effectively because you know what you need to do, especially in this fast paced world we live in.

I will teach you some specific steps in how to handle and deal with your stress.

Dealing effectively does not mean trying to eliminate stress. It is impossible to do that, still have an effective role in the world, and accomplish great things in your life. Stress will never disappear into outer space, so we need to learn how to live with it and lessen its impact upon us. The important thing is to *manage* stress.

Being stressed out weakens you mentally and physically. When you are weakened emotionally, your immune system is weakened. This causes you to get sick. The more stress you have, the more times you will get sick. Stress also causes many other unwanted symptoms.

Burnout is a serious outcome of being stressed over long periods. I know you've probably had times when you just couldn't face another day at work or some other pressure. But usually that feeling goes away. When you don't deal with stress, however, that feeling builds and builds until you suffer from burnout. Here is a quick overview of the signs of burnout and some remedies you can apply if you have these. After listing these, I will get into some methods in handling stress effectively so that it does not "handle you."

Signs of burnout (as described by the Truby Achievement Center):

- Desire to escape
- Indecision
- Erratic or incongruent emotions
- "Don't care" attitude
- Fatigue
- Dissatisfaction with *everything*
- Feeling out of control
- Decreased motivation
- Physical problems: heart palpitations, recurrent or lingering sickness, chest pains, and allergies

The Truby Achievement Center says, "Stress is not what you experience in life, it is your response to what you experience in life." If you understand where stress originates, which is in your mind, you can get past your stress very quickly.

Here are some remedies for burnout the Truby Achievement Center recommends:

1) Taking "time out"
2) Seeking counseling
3) Paying attention to your physical health
4) Assuming less responsibility
5) Learning and doing relaxation exercises

It may be hard at first as you start to work on these steps in handling and dealing with your stress, but with ongoing work and effort you will notice a difference in how you react to in particular and life in general. As you keep on doing it, it will become second nature and you will be able to live life managing stress rather than letting stress mangle you. This is truly living with peace.

Soon you will be able to handle any stressful situation. Remember that stress is not what happens to you, it is what happens within you.

There is both good stress and bad stress. It is not always the "bad" things that can cause you stress. What do I mean by good stress?

Well, let's say you are planning to go to college, or planning a vacation. That is all good and fun but can also cause stress for you. If you don't know how to manage that "good stress," it can have the same negative impact on your life as negative stress.

Methods for dealing with and handling stress (Some are Truby Achievement Center techniques):

1) Relaxation

Here is a technique I use to get relaxed about a situation. Picture yourself in a beautiful place—for instance in the mountains. Close your eyes and take deep breaths, breathing through your nose. Mentally put yourself in the picture you are imagining while you do the breathing. You can think of relaxation as taking deep breaths and mentally stepping away from the situation.

Here's an example:

I know a gentleman who was driving to work and got a flat tire. Instead of being calm, he ranted and raved at his friend in the car. He yelled, screamed and cussed. Now he has two problems on his hands. He has damaged his friendship, and he still has the problem with the car. Had he stepped out of the situation with an emotional time out, he would have avoided damaging the friendship. Think of stress as an aftershock. As trouble arises and you get stressed, more problems will come, in bigger and stronger amounts.

2) Be objective, not subjective

Being objective about a stressful situation can be simple if you adopt this attitude: Imagine that you are a bystander watching yourself in your stressful situation. You are there talking to your friend getting a little stressed and by being objective you can look at yourself talking with your friend. This is kind of weird but when you do it, you will gain control of your emotions instead of letting them control you.

Being subjective means getting really immersed in the conversation, which gets you emotional and defensive. People who are subjective end up saying something personal to their friend, and then will start fighting about that personal attack even though it was not an important part of the conversation in the first place.

Have you ever come upon a heated conversation between two people and you were standing there saying to yourself, "Why are these two people getting mad about something so insignificant? It seems so minor." That is what you want to do with your own stressful or potentially stressful interactions with others. By being objective, you can take your personal feelings out of the interaction.

Three things to do when you want to be objective:

- First, relax.
- Do not react to circumstances but instead think about the overall goal.
- And take yourself mentally out of the situation.

3) Exercise

You should exercise on a regular basis because regular exercise has tremendous benefits including:

- It makes you healthier.
- It releases endorphins that make you feel good and create mood stability.
- It is one of the seven areas of life that need to be fulfilled.

To be healthy in life, it is necessary to do some sort of exercise each day. Personally I have found that just one hour of workout will bring many hours of productive and effective work.

You try it ... when you work out, do you feel better and have more energy? Of course you do. Most importantly, have fun and enjoy your workouts because from your laughter you create endorphins that help you become even happier in life.

4) Exercise your options as well as your body: You do have a choice

Remember that there is more than one option or one way to do anything. You can change strategies if you need to. You can even change switch careers. You can make a choice to do something that doesn't stress you out as much. If you are stressed out working at one restaurant, then try working at another. You do have the power to make choices.

You don't have to be rigid in your thinking. Be open to choices and options and make a change in your life if that's what you need to do in order to reduce stress.

5) Develop a healthy self-esteem

It is critically important to develop a healthy self-esteem so when a boss or a friend says something to you, it won't stress you out. With a healthy self-esteem you are more ready to recognize that "everything is just input." It is just input you can accept … or can throw away. You will live life more fulfilled and happier by being proactive with a confident stance instead of a passive stance. Don't be arrogant or boastful; just have a stance that shows your beliefs.

6) Do something fun

Take time to do things that are fun for you. Take a vacation or go out to the park and relax as you read a book. Doing something you enjoy helps you live a balanced life.

7) Develop a positive attitude and perspective towards stress

Have the mind set that stress is a given. You will have stress all of your life, but it is how you react to it that determines if you will be a success. Make stress more of a game. In fact, you should enjoy having stress because it challenges you to overcome it. Be at peace when stressful times come, so you can laugh and be happy and be effective in dealing with stressful situations when they do arise.

8) Look beyond immediate results; look to the future

Look to the long term, not the short term. Most stressful situations affect you only in the short term if you handle them effectively because stress is what happens inside, not what happens to you. The longer you let stress and stressful situations affect you, the more "bad" outcomes will come from it in both the short and long terms.

When you are stressed, be able to take yourself out of the situation and look to the long haul. Ask yourself, "Should I even be getting stressed now? What are the consequences of getting stress? Will the stress hurt me in the long run? If so, I should not let this affect me and be stressed at this time."

There are additional ways to handle stress but these are the most powerful ones that have worked for me. Hopefully they will work for you.

Don't forget, life and successful attainment of your dreams is not about the absence of stress. It is about handling and dealing with stressful situations as they arise and not allowing them to overtake and overpower your dreams.

Make the decision to overcome your stress!

Chapter 7

"Now ...

... it's about action."

In this chapter you will learn:
- Gaining insight for the future;
- Developing actions that are consistent and ongoing;
- Applying what you have learned.

Now what? What are you going to do with this book? Are you going to just put it on the shelf with the others, or are you going to implement what you have learned and apply it to your life?

Now, it's about action. It's about getting it done. There are so many possibilities and opportunities you can accomplish in life. Search for them, find them, and accomplish them.

Take bits and parts of the information you have read and apply them every day and you will succeed. Your success is about ongoing, persistent action that leads toward your individual dreams. So, I recommend you go back if you need to, and focus for a week or so on each chapter, and apply it to your daily life.

After you have finished the first chapter go on to the next chapter and refresh and implement, and so on. You will not achieve everything you want, but I know—and promise—you will never achieve anything you don't first want.

Success takes time and effort, but when you plan your future with vision that encompasses your life purpose, you *will* be successful. However you define success, I believe this book can and will help you get there.

Setting goals is easy and fun, but it is not simple. It is easy to set goals, but the challenge and difficulty is in accomplishing them. It takes persistence, and it takes ongoing work.

You might work hard and you might need to make changes in your life to accomplish what you want. You might need to make changes that you don't want to make, but if you want to succeed, you *must* make them. They might point toward eliminating something in your life you like to do. But if you want to succeed, you must make the changes.

All successful people have taken risks in their lives. Some risks prove to be beneficial and others are not. The difference between an achiever and someone who fails is the willingness to take risks with the unknown.

Everything in life worth achieving involves risk, but when you succeed it will be worth every risk you have taken.

Develop self-discipline in striving for your dreams and goals because this makes you your own trainer in life. Your discipline is held in your daily actions.

Let's review the chapters. What have we learned?

Chapter 1 was about why it is important to believe, because without belief you will never have a chance to succeed. Self-esteem creates a greater belief in yourself because you know now it is not what you have done in the past that makes you a worthwhile person. It is solely who you are without your accomplishments.

If you don't have your "why" (that is the important reason to believe in your dream), you will probably not keep on going, even if you could, because you won't want to. You need to develop a mind set of "Possibility Thinking" because without it you will not see the many ways of accomplishing your dreams and because of that you won't succeed.

Chapter 2 stressed the importance of planning. Without a plan you don't know where you are going. In planning your life, you should begin with the end in mind. I gave you some ideas for finding your life purpose and from that life purpose developing and planning a life direction that is determined by your dreams and effective goals. In doing your planning, you need to be flexible in your goals because sometimes you might need to adjust or change one of the five aspects of setting goals to be effective. You can't be rigid in your thinking. Life brings challenges that might hold you back, so be flexible in adjusting to them so that in the end you attain your dream.

Chapter 3 taught the concept of reviewing your goals on a regular basis. Doing so creates focus and happiness. You have the option of adjusting your goals by adding something, changing something, or deleting something as you review them on a regular basis. But one of the most important actions you need in achieving your goals is to persevere and persist towards your goals until you reach them.

Chapter 4 showed ways to help you keep focused on your target with the help of a mentor or coach. You can always do more as a team than by yourself. It is vital in achieving big things in life to have a coach or a mentor. Having a coach or a mentor keeps you accountable and makes your goals clearer and simpler. Sometimes the coach will say what you *need* to hear, even if you might not *want* to hear it. If you do not have someone in mind to be your coach, you can come to me. That is my passion.

Chapter 5 describes how we all need to enjoy the process of life because we only get one time on earth, so we need to enjoy it. Life is an unending process, so enjoy the process by making sure you live balanced in all the seven areas of life.

Chapter 6 spoke about how to overcome obstacles by developing a flow chart. Combined with Chapter 1, this allows you to see that the roadblocks you encounter are just that: short term obstacles that you can overcome because you are a worthwhile person regardless of your past history or accomplishments. Success—and life—is not about the absence of problems; they are about how you react to them.

Chapter 7 is this chapter, about how to have ongoing success, knowing that there are many possibilities, and that you need to remember to enjoy this process. Look at it like it's a game, challenging but fun.

I believe that one cannot change the world, but I know one person can go put a dent in it.

May God bless you on your Journey.

Ah, but a person's reach should exceed his grasp. Or what's a heaven for?
— Robert Browning

About the Author

Curtis J. Steen is a young entrepreneur and a sought after speaker at schools and businesses. Throughout his young adult years, he has consistently studied the attributes of leadership. He teaches students life skills and systems to make life easier, and with small businesses, he helps with business development.

He is the directing partner of Soaring Eagles—a division of the Truby Achievement Center. To meet Curtis is to understand his exuberance and passion, which obviously and readily comes from his heart. Curtis graduated in 2000 with many honors and leadership accolades throughout his life and from the University of California at Davis. He graduated with a degree in Managerial Economics. His community involvement, scholastic achievement, and leadership in football earned him recognition in the Student-Athlete Leadership Hall of Fame

Curtis understands how to set goals, reach dreams, and—more importantly—help others achieve success. Clients who receive his training and facilitation are beyond benefited; they are inspired and launched towards success!

Contact & Ordering Information

To contact Curtis Steen about being mentored, about the Soaring Eagles Division of the Truby Achievement Center, about business development seminars, or to order additional copies of this book, contact:

Curtis J. Steen

    Phone/fax/pager: 1 (800) 792-1262 *(toll free)*
    Website: www.soaringeaglesdivision.com
    E-mail: curtis@soaringeaglesdivision.com
    Address:
        CJS Training & Consulting
        An affiliate of the Truby Achievement Center
        P.O. Box 1440
        Mount Shasta, CA 96067

www.ingramcontent.com/pod-product-compliance
Lightning Source LLC
Chambersburg PA
CBHW020005050426
42450CB00005B/323